No Stone Unturned

by Phyllis Feia

To Chris,
The most wonderful
of Organ players!
Love!
Phyllis

i

ISBN 0-9747147-8-X

Published by:
MK Publications
420 E. St. Germain
St. Cloud, MN 56304
www.yourbookpublisher.net
800-551-1023

Distributed by:
Metamorphosis
222 3rd Avenue NE
St. Cloud, MN 56304
320-253-4876

Printed in the United States of America

Acknowledgements:

I wish to thank, first of all, the many customers of The Good Earth Co-op of St. Cloud, Minnesota, who asked if I'd ever considered making the essays I wrote for the Co-op Newsletter into book form – without whom I could not have had the propensity or courage to do so.

I owe a deep debt of gratitude to the Dr. Al Leja, Professor Emeritus in the Dept. of English Literature at St. Cloud State University, who has graciously and diligently critiqued all of these essays with deft skill and wisdom borne out of his many years of experience and vast knowledge in the literary field. He and his wife, Edie, are treasured friends. "A Chance to Dance" one of the following essays is a brief portrayal of their faith in God and acceptance of His will.

I wish to thank and applaud, my dear friend Caroline Bull, Psy.D. for typing, re-typing, as well as offering many valuable suggestions regarding form and phrasing – out of her experience as a writer and published poet. It was a labor of love on her part as we diligently fine-tuned the essays. I'm deeply grateful to her for the many, many hours she invested in this project.

I wish to acknowledge my friend, Marley Keller, RN, who also critiqued the first collection of essays that had been put in manuscript form. Her sensitivity to detail, and years of experience as a hospice nurse made me know that I could depend on her sensitive insight into our human nature, which many of these essays seek to portray.

I'm deeply grateful to my friend, Debbie Hartwig, for providing me with the gift and benefit of her skills in proofrreading the finished manuscript.

A heartfelt thank you to my friend, Arerny McGann for her artwork on the stones sprinkled throughout my book. I'm honored that the artist who was national winner of the junior duck stamp contest in 2001—among many other acknowledgments in the Arts would create the stones I needed for my book.

My deep appreciation to Neal King, the professional photographer of "King Photography", who gifted me with his photographic skills in the cover design.

Essays By Phyllis Feia

Forward

There comes a time in the life of a wanna-be writer when one discovers a type of Forum where one might have opportunity to express publicly one's personal thoughts, ideas, observations and philosophy of life. This discovery leads the would-be-writer into an arena that may help determine whether what one has to say has any merit for others to ponder...benefit by.

Such was my case when I became editor in the mid-eighties of the Newsletter at our local food co-op; The Good Earth. I also was the manager of this small, quaint member-owned health food store in St. Cloud, Minnesota.

It became an altogether splendid experience for me, as I became better acquainted with the members and customers as well as the volunteers that made up the co-op community. I found like-minded people—kindred spirits who were environmentally conscious—discerning and weighing options in regard to the health of our planet. There was a concern for the food they put on the family table as well as for the small, family-owned farms where they endeavored to grow their crops organically without chemicals or pesticides.

These were my kind of people and as I became better acquainted with them, I began to feel safe and comfortable enough to express some of my thoughts and observations that had lain dormant within me for so many years. Hermit crab-like, I put out my feelers to explore this new found territory

*Denial of Death by Ernest Becker

through the medium of pen and paper. To my surprise and delight I received favorable responses, and knew that I'd been able to influence the readers to think about and comment on what I'd written. I wrote about my thoughts, my observations often on intimate, personal levels and was met with responses on intimate, personal levels. I'd hear; "It made me remember something similar to what you were saying and I thought about it in a new light." Or, "I never looked at the way one eats a candy bar, before." Or just, "It made me think."

My desire has always been to stimulate thought both within myself and others. I find status quo unbearable! A line from T. S. Eliot's Four Quartettes comes to mind:

> "We must be still, and still moving
> Into another intensity
> For a further union, a deeper communion
> Through the dark, cold and empty desolation..."

I've received enough encouragement from the readers of the Good Earth Food Co-op Newsletter in the past eighteen years to reach critical mass in my confidence level. This burgeoning confidence has driven me into a vast hitherto unexplored territory beyond my previous experience and emboldened me to believe that this small collection of short essays may have enough merit to put into book form and publish. Do they have merit? Let the reader decide. "The most that anyone of us can do is to fashion something—an object or ourselves—and drop it into the confusion, make an offering of it, so to speak..."* And this I do now, do at this time in my life—my life that spans seven decades.

Preface

Putting the Pieces Together

In April I attended a workshop at St. Benedict's Spirituality Center. I came away from that workshop feeling hinged with fragile thread. The subject was "Writing Your Life Story; Memoir as Prayer." The presenter was Patricia Hampl. I want to share a few choice fragments from the whole rich fabric of the workshop.

I've often thought of writing my life story, if only to take the fragmented pieces of my life, sort them out and stitch them together in orderly fashion, and see what I've got. To see what kind of pattern I came up with from all the varied and multi-colored experiences that went into the making of what I call *My Life*.

After some discussion on the subject of whether writing one's life story may be considered a self-absorbed, self-indulgent activity, we were able to shed such inhibitions and move on. We were instructed to take a clean sheet of paper and write as much as we could in ten minutes. We all had a story to tell, and there was no evidence of writer's cramp among the 50 people who attended the workshop. One can easily fill up one page in the allotted ten minutes, I found...even more!

The next step was being asked to volunteer to read the stories we'd written. Several brave souls shared their story, some with a slight, apologetic disclaimer regarding their styles and other uncertainties they experienced when it came to sharing one's own story with a not so small but intimate group of people. Brave Souls! I was a coward.

My ten-minute story lay before me on the desk as I listened with rapt attention to the readers of their own stories, glad that it was optional, rather than obligatory!

I was stunned at the contents of my ten-minute story as it lay there before my eyes. It needed my attention, as questions began to arise at what I had written and what I had not written.

But, with Patricia Hampl's skill and wisdom, we moved on to the next stage to answer such questions as; 1. What frightens you about your story? 2. What troubles you? 3. What surprises you?

I wasn't alone at being frightened, troubled and surprised. Many others responded to those questions. I, quietly in my own thoughts, was much too shaken by the things that frightened, troubled, and surprised me. I felt very, very shy. Some expressed concern that they hadn't, in the ten-minute period, mentioned people who were nearest and dearest to them as they wrote their stories.

"That's not unusual." Patricia counseled us, and offered the opportunity for the next state of writing—revision. We were offered the opportunity to write about the things that frightened, troubled, and surprised us.

I began to feel unhinged by that stage, but in a good way. The workshop I'd chosen to attend, I began to realize, was having a powerful impact. My memories were being quickened as tools were being supplied through the deft skill of the presenter as I was invited to look at my life in a new light as I began to plummet into new and unexplored realities of the life with which I'd thought I was so familiar.

Patricia spoke often that evening of the fragments of our lives...moments...the scraps which goes into the making of a quilt... the fragments of material left over from skirts, trousers, and shorts, shirts and dresses, jackets and blouses and the many various memories within those fragments. All separate pieces, but eventually finding their way into a patchwork quilt that brings warmth and comfort.

I think I shall get busy and make my 'quilt.' I believe I've collected quite enough fragments by now.

(Patricia Hampl has authored the following books: <u>Virgin Time</u>, <u>Spillville, A Romantic Education, I Could Tell You Stories</u>.)

Dedication

To my granddaughter Stephanie,

who posed the question,

"What's life all about, Grandma?"

No Stone Unturned

by Phyllis Feia

The 'Vision'

At one point in time my family and I lived in southern California in the little town of Bloomington. Bloomington was situated between San Bernadino on the north and Riverside on the South, and was nestled in the foothills of the San Bernadino Mountain Range.

The highest peak of the San Bernadino Mountain Range was Mount San Gorgonio, which rose, snow-covered and majestic, off in the distance from our home. Whenever I walked out to the mailbox, down our driveway to the other side of Eighth Street on which we lived, I always caught sight of Mount San Gorgonio—ever changing in its appearance depending on the atmosphere. I loved those walks to behold the beauty of that glorious mountain.

At times our family would venture out in the direction that would bring us to the mountain, leaving behind the dry, hot desert in which we lived, to play in the snow higher up in the mountain range.

What amazed me most, as we traveled the road that led to the great mountain, was the way, it would, at times, disappear out of sight as we followed bends and curves in the road. And then it would, again, emerge into our field of vision—shockingly majestic in its sovereign beauty.

The first time I traveled that road I was quite taken back at the appearance and the disappearance of that impressive sight. Each time it became larger to my eyes, I'd think, there's no way I could lose sight of it again! But then, at the

1

next turn, it would suddenly vanish. I'd wonder, how is this possible? How can such an enormous panoramic vision seem to dematerialize? And yet, time after time, that's just what it did!

When we finally reached our destination we'd become 'at one' with the mountain. Though we were far from its summit, it was no longer the mountain I'd seen from the distance when I walked to our mailbox. It was no longer so spectacularly immense. In traveling toward our goal we found ourselves 'identified' with that goal—but not forgetting the vision we'd had at the beginning of our journey.

If you have a love of the metaphor as I do, you've no doubt received the 'message'—as I did, on those journeys to the Mountain…and how sometimes when we set out on our individual journeys toward a distant goal we need not lose heart when the 'vision' we first had is lost for a time. Take heart from my story and the metaphor there in.

The Heart's Treasure

I'd like to tell you a little of my story—my early years—and how the depression that hit our country around 1929 affected my family…and me.

My parents, four sisters and two brothers lived on a farm in the area of Randal, Minnesota where I was born in 1932.

Many years later I learned that my parents had lost the mortgage on that farm. We moved from that farm to another farm south of Little Falls when I was four years old. My father's brother owned this farm. At least part of the agreement for us to live there was that my father helped my uncle build a house, barn and outbuildings on another piece of land where my uncle and his wife would live.

Consequently we had been poor. But I knew nothing of that for many years. Our basic needs were met because we lived off the land, as many people did in those days. Anything store-bought was a luxury; fresh fruit was a rare treat, as was lunchmeat and store-bought bread that I craved when I saw kids at school having such a rare treat for lunch. How I envied those 'lucky' kids!

The clothes I wore were hand-me-downs from twin cousins a couple years older than me. I was happy with the hand-me-downs, but was thrilled beyond words when my mother bought me a brand new outfit. Between the ages of six and fourteen, I had three new outfits. But I didn't feel deprived, nor did I ever beg for new clothes.

There was never any discussion that I can remember between my parents over our financial state. Whatever they said about it was private—between them, and them alone. But I did hear much discussion about the war—World War II. I was nine years old when Japan bombed Pearl Harbor on December 7, 1941. I knew that something very bad had happened to our world that Sunday, fifty-one years ago…very bad and very frightening. It was a time when my brother Harold, who was in the National Guard, was inducted into the military service and one of the first to leave our quiet rural area. I remember watching from our kitchen window as he walked lone down the dirt road toward Little Falls—walked away to War. I felt sad and forlorn. Harold was a good brother, fourteen years older than me, at twenty-three years old.

During the war there was rationing. We were issued rationing books that had a certain amount of coupons depending on the number of family members. There were many things that were rationed, such as sugar, chocolate, canned goods, paper, rubber, gas, coffee, cigarettes, and a number of other things. This put many restrictions on our already limited food supply. The greatest problem for me was the restriction on sugar which meant that my mother could make few cakes, cookies, and pies; our family's treats. That hurt! And then there was that large emptiness of my brother's absence and the worry over what would happen to him.

Adolph Hitler loomed as a great threat to our world. So great was that threat in my mind that I felt he would be in our world forever. I remember looking in a magazine at a picture of a little girl about my age who held a magazine picture of Hitler. She was pointing at him as she looked up at her mother as she posed the question, "Mom, who was Hitler?" This picture was designed to depict some future time when the world was free of this man. I'm reminded of a song, written during this time. It went, "There'll be bluebirds over the white cliffs of Dover, tomorrow; when the world is free. There'll be love and laughter, and peace ever after, tomorrow just you wait and see…" I couldn't imagine a time when anyone would ever need to ask, "Who was Hitler?"

Eventually the war was over. My brother returned home. He'd been away for seven years and he had traveled to many countries: Italy, Ireland, and Africa. He had many stories to tell and other stories to forget.

This portion of my story is about as short as I could make it in this limited space in order to tell you how I've learned to value what is important in life, and how I've learned to be thankful for the simple things of life. And how my appreciation for simple things of life comes from having too little rather than too much. Having too little made me more aware of the truth that "the best things in life are free." The "best things" are what money can't buy. The "best things" are the treasures of the heart; the love of friends and family, the beauty of Creation, thankfulness, generosity, kindness, forgiveness, and peace. These are the Greatest Gifts, and they are free—but "costing not less than everything" (T. S. Eliot).

The Wisdom of the Master Gardener ...
A Lesson in Pruning

Four years ago I lost a very dear, long-time friend to cancer. At that time I'd purchased a Hibiscus, which became a symbolic reminder of my friend. Those of you who are familiar with the blossoms will understand when I tell you how very much I enjoyed each 'unfolding'—so beautiful that they often drew tears. I beheld their loveliness, and remembered my friend and how she'd un-folded in her personal growth, leading up to the time of her death.

A year ago, last spring, I decided to plant that beautiful Hibiscus in the ground for the summer, little realizing what a mistake I was making by doing so. How it flourished throughout the summer months! I'd never seen it look so beautiful! But after I dug it up in the fall, re-potting it in a larger pot to accommodate its summer growth, I was dismayed to watch the leaves turn yellow and fall—leaving only bare stems by mid-winter. I was, however, determined to keep it alive, although I'd begun to lose hope by the time spring arrived as so little fresh growth had begun to adorn the bare stems.

I didn't want that beautiful plant to die! Nor could I bear to look at the bare 'spindles' that had once borne on abundant amount of glossy leaves and vivid blossoms. I made a decision to prune it back, radically, in the hope that the pruning shears might trigger a response in the roots. I was also ready to accept the possibility that it might die. But, to my great delight, shortly thereafter, fresh new growth began to emerge all along the remaining stems. Throughout the summer it put forth more and still more leaves and blossoms. Never, in the past three years, had there been such abundant growth! I behold it every single day, as it keeps putting forth its beautiful and abundant blossoms—so thankful that I'd been moved to cut back those poor, dead-looking spindles.

Metaphorically there's been a pruning lesson for me on a deeper level. I've realized that the wisdom of the 'Master Gardener' has been at work at various times in my life to prune me, lest I become spindly and in order to trigger a response from my roots; in the depths of my being, and send forth new life, Heartier Life (Life from the Heart). I find that pruning is a good thing, although it isn't always certain whether one might survive. It is the ultimate gift bestowed on me by the Master Gardener. It contributes to a deeper, richer, sturdier life. At least, that's been my experience. And so I can say in all honesty and gratitude; "Thanks, I needed that." And so can my Hibiscus, if it could speak.

The Unforeseeable Future

hat will the coming year bring?" I always wonder, as I put away my Christmas decorations. I've wondered that every year for at least half of my life. And then, as I've taken the decorations out each year. I reflect on what the past year has brought. My son, Les, Called it "Marking Time." For him marking time was yearly visits to the North Shore on Lake Superior.

Even as I write this in late October 2002, I wonder; What will the next two months bring, before anyone else reads what I write today. I seem to have this engrained notion that I can't take anything for granted. One thing that this notion does is to cushion the shock if something tragic happens in my life or in the lives of people close to me. It seems we've all experienced more shocks than usual every since September 11, 2001—and we live in a constant state of uncertainty—in this Nation of ours and this World of ours.

And yet, I've often thought that those who believe life should be something we have control over from day to day, week to week and year to year are living with an illusion. Yes, we do have a certain amount of control over our lives through the choices we make. However, when a bolt of tragedy strikes and stark reality of the truth that not 'everything' is within our control is brought home to our senses, there is often great resistance. There are questions; "why?" and "why me?" and "why us?" But very rarely do I hear someone respond to personal tragedy with some realization that "what has befallen me, us, my family, my friends, my nation has happened countless times to others—and to their families and friends and nations." I wonder why can't people realize this truth? Instead of asking, "Why?" why not think, "so this is what it's like! So this is what countless others have been experiencing for eons of time—and now I'm 'in' on the experience—and my pain is only a part of a greater pain."

The attitude one brings to any tragedy that befalls can make such a difference in how the suffering is borne. Does one wonder; "Where was God in all this?" My question is, "Did we question God's role when tragedy struck in the lives of others we didn't know, in other countries of the world, at other times in history?" If not, why not? Maybe because we would need to ask that question every single day, every hour, every minute, every second. Or maybe because it's too shockingly different when tragedy strikes home because we think we didn't deserve to have this happen to us...or our family member...or my friend or my Nation. And how do we get to decide who deserves what? Although one cannot always be conscious of the suffering of one's fellow human beings, when tragedy strikes, one can open one's heart a little more...care a little more...pause a little more...hold one's fellow-sufferers in our thoughts a little more. "Lord, Teach us to care, and not to care. Teach us to sit still...."

You Must Be Present To Win

e've survived yet another Minnesota winter. Now, as we continue to move out of the cold, sterile climate of winter into the warm, fertile climate of spring and summer, we welcome this change. Though most of us have a preference regarding our favorite season, we Minnesotans all seem to appreciate this change from the icy, cold barrenness of winter to the freshness and warmth of spring.

The changing of seasons symbolizes turning points within ourselves. Because we are familiar with the changing seasons we know what's coming next and, therefore, make ourselves ready. Changing seasons, also, represent a new beginning, a marking of time, and a time for reflection on the past year. Because we expect this change, we accept it; we make ourselves ready for it and welcome it.

Acceptance of change is characteristic of the awakened mind and heart. As one is desirous of personal growth, change is inevitable just like the changing seasons and the process, thereof. Without this understanding of change we can easily become frightened by life's changes, the inevitable losses and disappointments, the insecurity we experience, our aging and death. Misunderstanding leads us to fight for or against life, run from pain and grasp at security and pleasures that can never be truly satisfying.

Instead of growth and blossoming with change, we may tend to create conflict through resistance. We see in our lives the constant element of likes and dislikes and a fight to resist all that frightens us. We see how much our struggle with life keeps our hearts closed.

Letting go of our personal battles and opening our hearts to things as they are helps us to live in the moment and come to rest in the moment! A sign in a casino which says, "You must be present to win," gives us a clue that leads us to understand at what point the "blossoming" takes place. When we come into the Present, life blossoms, both within and around us. We are apt, also, to encounter that Truth we've been working so hard to avoid. Maybe we can look upon that Truth as the rich manure in our lives that brings forth fruition. But we must have courage to face whatever truth presents itself: our pain, our shame, our desires, our grief, our losses, our lives, everything that touches and moves us deeply.

Living fully brings within ourselves wholeness. Allowing all truth to have expression may become the richest possible experience of our lives. And with these changing seasons of our lives, we can shed the old and embrace the new.

...More Than Food...

I n our search toward Wholeness, we must become more attentive for those things which tend to throw us off balance. Often, one's first thought is, "What have I eaten?" And often times it may well have been something in the category of food, fumes or toxic substances. But we must continue, also, to look behind the symptoms for other things that produce stress and, consequently, throw us off balance.

In the May newsletter, we addressed the fear of, and resistance to, the change that produces stress and is often the factor that weakens our immune system.

There is another universal factor that produces stress in our lives. That is the expectations and standards we hold for others, be it family, friends, and/or colleagues, and the expectations and standards they hold for us. These expectations and standards foisted upon us begin when we are born, and do not necessarily end at death.

Whether overtly voiced or not, parents set behavior standards for their children. Children, as they grow and develop, have expectations of their parents. This is also true of teacher and student, employer and employee. We say, overtly, "This is the person I want you to be." We reinforce this by 'affirmation' or the lack thereof. To a certain degree, there is nothing wrong with expectations and standards held for us by others and vice versa. But it becomes a source of stress when other people's standards for us diminish our own individuality, when we find ourselves questioning how we make our own choices. And although we are greatly in need of others' perspective, advice and opinions, we may also hope our friend, family member, or colleague will, in the end, give us 'permission' to make our own decision.

We must also remember this is a two-way street. Stress can build as we deny our own individuality in favor of winning another's approval. Therefore, when one finds an imbalance that reveals itself in mental and physical symptoms, let us not stop at the point of the tangible, such as food and other substances, but look, also, beyond the obvious into the realm of the mind-body connection, and investigate the possible cause of imbalance or in other words "illness".

Wholeness constitutes freedom. A well-rounded individual is Free and others feel freedom in their presence. Freedom begets freedom.

Let us give consideration to this area of our lives, this 'center' out of which we have the opportunity to express our true selves.

A Time to Remember...

No one needs to be told we're living in a time of materialism and consumerism, of lost values and a shift in ethical standards. We find ourselves tempted to return to old values and ways. But can we go back?

Or does the answer to our dilemma lie, not in the past nor in the future, but within?

Times are changing, and we seem to be losing parts of ourselves along the way, in the process of change. Like the straw man in the Wizard of Oz, we've been pulled apart and "There's a piece of me here and a piece of me there!"

Our personal identity is being threatened or lost in the shuffle as we strive to live by the current standards, and instead of identifying ourselves by saying, "I am _____", we say what we do. We tend to label everything, including ourselves. We think we know who we are through job identity rather than through our personal history. Because we know the name of a thing we think we know what it is…this applies to how we view ourselves and others.

But the truth is the "fate and character of each of us is borne in mystery…our individuality so hidden and profound that it takes a lifetime for identity to emerge."*

One way for us to seek our identity is to return to our childhood memories and reclaim that remote part of our identity. In that child we have hopes and dreams, fears and uncertainties, laughter and spontaneity, honesty and openness. "That child who is eternally present in our thoughts and dreams may be full of weakness and faults, but that is who we are." *

Since this is a time of the year we often focus on the child, let us reacquaint ourselves with that child within. Let us get out the

*Excerpts from: Care of the Soul by Thomas Moore

14

pictures...reflect and remember... and maybe we can share our story. Let this be a time for turning within and reflecting.

Maybe, as we unwrap some treasured memories we'll stumble across some of the values and dreams we lost along the way, and reclaim some missing parts of ourselves.

Kindness – A Noble Weapon

o doubt, almost everyone has become acquainted with the term "random acts of kindness" as I have. However, hearing the term and experiencing the act itself, is like the relationship between a snapshot of an individual and the individual in person.

Many random acts of kindness have been performed on me throughout my lifetime. These are the unexpected, unsolicited favors bestowed by friend, acquaintance, or stranger. The prerequisite for such a favor is that it was unexpected...random.

A customer bestowed one of these *random acts of kindness* upon me last week by sharing the book Random Acts of Kindness with me, however I don't think this was *random* but intended kindness. My heart was warmed. My soul was inspired. My memory began to recall many random acts of kindness that never got into the news. Sometimes they're passed on by word of mouth, sometimes not. Sometimes they are forgotten by the recipient, as the focus of thoughts

15

gravitate toward the negative aspects of life and the world. Isn't "no news good news" after all? Therefore, we tend not to share the good news while we focus on the bad.

What we really need is balance. Balance corresponds to wholeness. And aren't we all somewhat starved to hear the good news, in the midst of all the acts of crime and violence, or in the midst of the long and bitterly cold winter, or in the midst of the strife within families, businesses, institutions, nations, the world?

Good and kind deeds expressed from one ordinary, average individual to another might be a missing nutrient in our 'diet' as those deeds are shared with each other, as little morsels of spiritual nourishment.

Taking Time for Silence

My experience of semi-retirement in these past sixteen months has been so rich and full I wish to encourage those who can to take the "leap." And for those many who cannot, I encourage you to allow yourself whenever possible space for reflection…time to just be still and listen to your inner voice.

To those who have inquired of me how I like the semi-retirement, I respond in glowing terms: "I love it!" My life isn't so structured. There's time for more of a free flow...for sitting in the sun, for getting in touch with my self.

One day, while kneading my bread, I thought of how I loved working with this malleable dough, shaping it into loaves, and how each time I make bread I'm creating. This bread making time is also an opportunity to reflect. Thinking comes easy when you're kneading bread, watering plants, sewing. All of these various activities feed and nourish me deeply. They satisfy me. I realize how few people there are who have remained in touch with the things that bring such rich satisfaction. Under great pressure of time, of duties and commitments, we seem to have forgotten what it is that used to bring joy. There's hardly the time or inclination to reflect on one's present circumstances and pose the question: "Is this what I really want?" It takes time and space to allow the question to rise to surface consciousness.

We are not skilled in the inner life where desire, hopes and dreams flourish, take root and grow, because we've left ourselves so little time to cultivate that inner life. We've tried to be many selves all at once, without all these selves being organized by a single Mastering Life within us. We too easily follow the common Western method of making a quick decision amid conflicting claims within us.

Over the margins of life comes a whisper, a faint call, a premonition of richer living we know is passing us by. Strained by the mad pace of our daily outer burdens, we are further strained by inner uneasiness because we have hints that there is a way of life vastly richer and deeper than this harried existence—and we're missing that experience.

"If only we can slip over into the Center! If only we can find the silence that is the source of sound."

Pushing the Pause Button

owadays I hear a lot about "channel surfing" the sport of holding the remote control to the TV and pushing the buttons, going from channel to channel. I understand that some people will try to watch two programs at the same time by switching back and forth from one channel to the other.

Here is another symptom or "side-effect" of this Age of Technology. No wonder many people have such a short attention span. They carry the channel surfing habit into real life. "If I'm bored, I'll switch the channel," and ZAP! You've lost their attention as they tune you out and start thinking about what's on another channel. People who practice this channel surfing are missing the moment. Little do they know how much they may be missing.

I do not have a remote control on my television. I do, however, have a remote control for my VCR. I have often used it to backtrack and replay something I wasn't able to grasp the first time through. For slower thinkers like myself, life flies by much too swiftly. I like to replay a lot of things. Not only do I want to replay, but I also have a great capacity for desiring to re-run portions of my life.

We used to talk about turning back the pages of time and rewriting some of the script. This desire to rewrite is often born out of regrets over our own actions based on limited understanding at the time. As I grow older, and hopefully wiser, I look back sorrowfully. "If only I had known then what I know now..." is the constant lament. But I didn't know and so much of what I did or didn't do was a result of ignorance...plain, unabashed, unadulterated ignorance!

But I've learned I can forgive myself for the ignorance of the past, and by forgiving myself, I find a great degree of resolution. Not only does my own forgiveness benefit me, but it benefits others around me. When I learn to be kind and forgiving toward myself, I tend to spread that forgivingness around me. As I become more tolerant of myself, I become more tolerant of others. I also find that I'm able, more and more, to live in the moment, as the unresolved issues of my life have been addressed. Otherwise, unresolved issues have a way of haunting one, like ghosts of the past, ghosts that we keep trying to avoid by distractions, by channel surfing...by various forms of activity...by filling up our time in many various ways that we never have those moments when one can just, so to speak, push the pause button and allow oneself the time and space to truly see and feel and respond to that which is in need of one's undivided attention.

Don't Miss the Dance

So often we find that life yields to us bittersweet experiences if we are willing to attune ourselves to the full meaning when tragedy strikes our lives, or when tragedy strikes another, and we experience its touch.

Such is the case of the young police officers who died in the line of duty this past month. While their death became a public affair because of the roles they played as protectors of others, many hearts were touched as portions of their lives unfolded and came to light, revealing their courage and commitment.

One officer was quoted by his fellow officer who remembered a line from a song by Garth Brooks, "If you avoid the pain, you'll miss the dance," in connection with the way that this young police officer had lived his life and had left this legacy to his friend. It was, indeed, touching to hear this line being quoted and attributed to one who had lived *into* the pain.

Pain comes to all. Pain is no respecter of persons. We often times have no choice in the matter if pain comes to visit in our lives. We do, however, have a choice whether we reject and resist, or whether we accept and bear it. In resisting we learn nothing. In accepting we may learn what it has come to teach us, and what we learn may bring us down avenues that lead to a fuller and richer life, a life that touches others' lives for the good.

I'm reminded of one Co-op shopper who has touched my life through her pain. She is a woman in her mid-seventies. Through the years she has greeted me warmly, expressing genuine interest in how I was doing. Often times she'd kiss me on the cheek as she greeted me. She had sparkle, radiating life in all directions.

I hadn't seen her for quite some time, when one day her husband came in to shop. I enquired about Edith. He told me she had her leg amputated below the knee due to problems with circulation. He was not at all morose as he told of the situation, and told me of how well she was doing. And so was he!

Then one day, a few weeks later, Edith and her husband, Al, came into the store, radiant as ever. She was on crutches while one leg of her white slacks dangled loose. She was "coming along fine," she said, and looking forward to being fitted with a prosthesis, and anticipating eventually taking up her tennis game. My heart welled up within me as she spoke of how much better she was feeling with that troublesome leg removed. She was frank and open, and she made it easy for me to ask questions and talk about it.

I was thoroughly inspired by the beautiful, heroic way in which Edith and Al had accepted this pain and lived into the experience with no shred of avoidance, denial, or self-pity.

I don't doubt that Edith will be dancing very soon, if not at this very moment!

Finding Our Path

I was recently re-reading one of my journals dated May 1990. The entire memory was triggered when I read the portion that told of my visit to a Jungian community in Three Rivers, Michigan. Because it had long ago been an apple-producing orchard, the community called Apple Farm covered a considerable number of acres. One afternoon I decided to go for a walk. I received instructions from one of the community members and set out on my journey. Here is a portion of my journal entry that day:

"I've just returned from quite a little adventure! One of the people working in the garden directed me to an area where I could take a lovely walk. As I followed her directions (or so I thought) I realized later I had missed the turn she'd told me of. After walking for an hour or so, I began to retrace my path and wend my way back. But it wasn't too long before I realized that the path I was on came back, full circle to the place I'd started. Then I saw what seemed like paths that led out from the circle, but they all narrowed down and disappeared. Part of me became alarmed. Part of me was at peace. I began to look for the meaning in this experience. And, as I continued to walk, I took in more than before the loveliness of the place. There was a lake in the distance covered with lily pads, but I was fearful of losing the 'circular' path on which I'd found myself, of having no path at all.

Then I began to think about paths as I continued to walk. I thought about how dependent we are on paths and how important it is to us that pathmakers make paths one can see! The path I'd been on had been a wide path, but had become narrower and narrower until I'd lost the security of being on a well-trodden path, and I couldn't find my way back to that well-trodden path of safety, certainty and predictability.

It was beginning to grow dark. I wondered when I would be missed by the people of the community. But then, maybe I wouldn't be missed, because we were allowed at that place to follow our own path...to do as we pleased...go where we wished to go...stay where we desired to stay. No schedule was imposed upon us, only offered.

Finally, I risked getting off the circular path and heading in the direction of the lake with the lily pads I found as I came closer to the lake, some outbuildings, a cottage, and then a dirt road! It would take me to some destination, regardless of which direction I chose. I would no longer be going in circles. The dirt road led me out of the woods to a paved road and the paved road led me eventually back to Apple Farm Community, which had been my destination." (End of journal entry.)

As I read this entry it struck me that all of us are on some path in life. Some of those paths I believe are circular. Some paths are leading us to a destination of our desire (at least we travel hopefully). Some paths are not really paths. They are only meadow and woods with nothing clearly marked to give us a clue as to our next step. These paths call us to follow our own heart and fall back on our own intuition toward our own unique destiny...our own personal calling and yet, we are not alone as we pursue such a path as this.

The Value of Ancient Wisdom

ave you ever experienced in your search for one thing; you "stumble across something of greater value than that which you were seeking?

This was my recent experience as I was looking through a number of books, I stumbled upon one that captured my attention: Living Biographies of Great Scientists by Henry Thomas and Dana Lee Thomas. The penciled in $3.00 mark on the front inside page told me I'd picked it up at a book sale, somewhere in the remote past. It drew my attention, and I put it aside from the rest of the pile. Later, when I made myself lunch, I carried it to the place where I chose to partake of my "vittles"…a place in the warm, spring sunlight.

The food that entered my mouth and satisfied my stomach was nothing compared to the food that entered my mind and energized soul and spirit. I read in the introduction: "The reader of Biography lives not one but many lives. For he expands his own experiences by adding to them the experiences of his fellow men. He sees the world, so to speak, through many pairs of eyes, and thus learns to contact his neighbors through many sympathetic chords of understanding."*

Being a lover of biographies, I could concur as I read on: "Every biography is a window which enables us to look at the world through different angles of reality."*

Living Biographies of Great Scientists by Henry Thomas and Dana Lee Thomas

My first scientist was Archimedes (287-212 B.C.) the man who coined the phrase "Eureka! Eureka! I have found it!" when he discovered a simple solution to a problem given to him by Hiero, King of Syracuse regarding the quality of his gold crown.

We often, in our modern technological age, think ourselves more intelligent than those who lived ages ago. Inflated egos only make us think we are. And, sad to say, we've become more dependent on machines than our own unlimited resources...the mind and the indomitable human spirit.

Archimedes defeated a Roman fleet with the use of "burning mirrors."* These mirrors were huge concave plates of metal so designed to focus the blazing light of the sun on the oncoming fleet. Archimedes also developed pulleys by which he could move a maximum of weight with a minimum of effort. With his invention he turned a fleet of sixty Roman vessels into a "handful of toys"* as they were picked up out of the water with enormous grappling hooks "straight into the air, and then plunged them, stern first into the depths."*

Archimedes developed many other valuable inventions that are in use today. Ancient writers tell us he was a "kindly, gentle man." His students idolized him and he, "quieted them like a father."*

When I read accounts of such people, I realized how desperately needy our own generation has become as a result of our pursuit of technology.

We need, "kindly, gentle" teachers who can guide us to develop our own abilities to learn grow, develop, intuit, and expand toward higher, better and less destructive ways of living our lives. We also need, now and then, a backward glance that draws on the legacies left us by great men and women of recent and ancient times, who can inspire us to use our very own, valuable resources; the intellect and the indomitable human spirit.

In Search of Meaning

esterday, my five year-old granddaughter, Stephanie asked me a question: "What's life all about?" Little did she know what a very big question she was asking. I've been working on this question myself for quite some time, many years in fact. It ties in, too, with the question, "Who am I?" as I pursue the answer to that question I may come closer to the meaning of life.

Life has so much to do with perception. I react to the negative philosophy underlying the song: *Life's A Bitch and Then You Die*. Something in me knows that there's no truth to that statement. One may feel sometimes that 'Life's a Bitch' but when we are able to separate fact from feeling, we can regain equilibrium and set our sights for meaning rather than meaninglessness.

One also learns, in life, to separate 'fact' from fancy and come to terms with the fact that life is not easy…it's tough. Life is like a training camp; it tests our mettle. In a former newsletter on the subject of death there was a quote from an article in the Utne Reader: "Unless one has faced death one cannot really face life." And people often say: "I don't want to get too close to anyone because I'm afraid if I do, I'll lose them."

But death comes in many ways other than the ultimate death. It comes to relationships. It comes to nations. It comes to the creative spirit. Therefore, to avoid disappointment, we often fear to attempt, fear to open ourselves up to others and become vulnerable, like a child. We may even fear to ask the question: "What is life all about?" for fear we might learn the answer, and we're afraid of what the answer might be.

Thoreau, in his essay: "Where I Lived and What I Lived For." says; "I went to the woods because I wished to live deliberately, to confront only the essential facts of life, and see if I could not learn what it had to teach and not, when I came to die, discover I had not lived."

So, what are those 'essential facts of life?' Maybe they're different for each one of us. To one it is the 'American Dream' of becoming a millionaire. To another it's learning to live off the land as simply as possible. To one it's to become famous and great, to another it's simply to serve others. To one it may be to have a BALL, to another it may be earning one's value through working hard and self-sacrificing. To many of us there are mixed bags when it comes to the meaning of life; to others there is not even a clue as to what life means.

We are passengers on the Planet Earth, whirling through space at a speed of 66,000 miles per hour. Each of us, as on a train, have our individual destinations.

One's goals, one's purpose for living is tied in with one's own personal identity, and gives some clue as to what life is all about. If the question is never asked, what then? Then it must be said of us, "we had the experience, but missed the meaning." As to how I answered Stephanie; I do not know what I said in response to her as I was somewhat shocked into speechlessness. I'm not sure what I would say if given time to think. There is an answer but how to define or confine it. Ah, there's the rub! Maybe the answer is too big.

A Time for Everything

Last September the Newsletter carried an article titled, "Cancer Spells Crisis." It told of my son Les' cancer. It told also about his choice of alternative therapy rather than orthodox medicine.

On Saturday, April 18th, Les died a very peaceful death, having suffered very little pain. Only in the last few days did the pain give him episodes of problems. He was very much alive and with us almost up to the end. He had no need for pain medication, having chosen an alternate means of pain management.

There were never any regrets on Les' part or on the part of the family for having chosen an alternative therapy. Whether the therapy, if religiously followed, would have benefited him in such a way as to promote his recovery is a question that cannot be answered. He was not able to stick with it as faithfully as we'd hoped. He did, however, alter his eating habits, considerably avoiding dairy products, meat, and most processed food.

Les lived his life so fully up to the very end that we all thought there could be a turn-around at any time. But when the last hours began to unfold, we who were close to him found ourselves more prepared than we'd thought.

Preparing for death is similar to preparing for life. "Before we can truly face life, we must face death." Death is not always an enemy, and often it comes to us on friendly terms.

However, for those who have not had ample opportunity to prepare themselves for the loss of someone close, death comes as an unwelcome intruder. For those of us close to Les, it was not an intrusion. We had much opportunity to acquaint ourselves with the possibility that we would be "visited" at some point. We made use of the time to prepare ourselves and to gather many precious memories. We are rich in our memories. And we are thankful for the time we were given—and yet there is the great pain of loss. Les will be greatly missed. He was a sensitive, kind, gentle, loving soul.

The Mystic Chords of Memory

emories and our relationship to them are often quite mysterious. Sometimes our memories stimulate a desire to return to the past...to live in the past. One word to describe such a feeling is nostalgia, which, according to Webster is: 1. the state of being homesick, a wistful or excessively sentimental...yearning for return to...some past period or irrecoverable condition."

These kinds of memories may be welcome or unwelcome, depending on how much pain they evoke. As we continue on our life's journey and memories return to us along the way, we find our evaluation of them changing, because we have learned to see things from a different perspective. Sometimes those memories become more precious to us, and sometimes they become of less value. Some we choose to tuck away in the Treasure Chest of our heart. Some we discard to the 'waste basket' of our lives where forgotten things belong. And there is, yet the 'other kind of memories. Like ghosts, they haunt us. They return unbidden. They fill us with shame and regret. They plague us. Our response, often, to such memories is to shut the door on them, turn up the volume, and busy ourselves in an effort to drown them out to drive them back into the deeper recesses of our mind.

This is how some people deal with grief and sorrow, as well. Its how some people deal with the agony over "the road not taken." It is, also, how some people deal with bad things that happened to them as a child or as an adult. This way of dealing with past memories includes regret over our own actions, as a child or adult. And, rather than turning and facing what is there to be faced, we become fugitives on the run, and we work hard to resist and repress those parts of our past that cast a shadow over the present, and try hard not to think about those things.

We cope by denial. As a result of this resistance, we become fragmented. In treating those memories like distant relations that we never see, it becomes impossible to be a 'whole' person. Only by opening ourselves up to these unwelcome memories, letting them have an audience, can we find ourselves, our whole, entire selves. Only then can we find true health: the condition of being sound in body, mind and spirit…flourishing.

> "Sometimes in the here and now
>
> My There and Then shows up.
>
> Generations appear in one body.
>
> I listen attentively,
>
> Wondering which will speak first." *

*'Grief; The Loss of Dreams'   by Ted Bowman

Great Expectations

As the Holidays begin to seem not too far off, the idea of 'expectations' comes to mind. We all have memories of some kind from our childhood and young adult years. Some of us have happy memories, some painful, and some just vague, mediocre memories of family and friends gathering together.

Whatever has been in our past experience seems to have great bearing on what we bring to our present situation. If they were good, happy and fulfilling, we, as adults, try to reproduce that experience again and again from year to year. But, the greater the expectations, the greater the disappointment if we fail in our efforts. If it was painful, we may bring such low expectations to our present situation that any attempt at entering into the 'Festive Spirit' is quite lame. No expectations, no disappointment.

This idea of expectations carries over into all areas of our lives. Wherever we go, we bring with us our expectations, or lack thereof. Some of us, being idealists, are looking for an ideal family, and ideal life, and ideal mate, and ideal friend. When life or people fail to produce that ideal for us, we are subject to great disappointment. Is the solution, then, to lower our expectations in order to avoid being disappointed? Would lowering of the expectations also diminish our enthusiasm? Enthusiasm can be a key contribution to every experience we might enter—making us more receptive to any new adventure.

And how, when others disappoint us, can we maintain a hopeful and enthusiastic outlook? And how, when we disappoint ourselves and our own expectations of ourselves, can we maintain a bright outlook that isn't laden with accumulated regret, and feelings of hopelessness?

We humans cope somehow on a regular daily basis with expectations and disappointments. But what can offer a better remedy in our lives than just coping is to face our disappointments squarely, asking, "Was there some meaning in this for me?" Maybe the experience brings with it a message of something of value that helps me better understand myself and others…and where I'm at and were to go from here lest I have the experience and miss the meaning.

And meaning we will always find when we open ourselves to the truth that each experience offers. Then all is not lost, even if we've invested great energy and hope in someone or something that disappoints us.

Instead of disappointment on the heels of Great Expectations with an outcry of "Everything went wrong…" we might say, "Well, now, just wait a minute here. Maybe things went just the way they were meant to go in order that we might find the meaning." Herein lies the unexpected good, the hidden treasure…that which may even exceed our paltry expectations, if we can only look for the meaning.

Turn of the Screw

One morning, in the recent past, I descended my basement stairs, armed with a screwdriver, to perform an overdue operation. My uncertainty in regard to my ability, and deep-rooted procrastination was overcome by the need of the moment. Removing the front panel of my electric water heater, I turned the screw that regulates the water temperature. It was such an easy and simple task, and yet...for some reason...I'd placed it in a very low position on my priority list.

Once this simple task was completed, my mind was flooded with questions of why I hadn't acted on this matter months—years ago, as a result of these questions, regarding my apparent stupidity, I began to ponder on the 'meaning.' Here was a perplexing aspect of the 'Human Condition" in which I find myself a typical participant. I marveled at my inconsistency and lack of frugality in one area of my life, while I pride myself on my frugality in other areas.

But my train of thought moved on and began to explore other areas of my life where I might be exhibiting inconsistencies. Areas of my life that wait for a little attention, small areas, easy to overlook and pass by while I take care of the really important things, and yet draining my resources.

Later, I talked the situation over with a friend. She, too, had experienced this problem when it was brought to her attention. She told of a latch on her back door that had been loose for months, requiring only a few turns of a screw, and yet had been neglected.

As we chuckled together over the folly of our disregard for the small things, we also hit upon the possibility of the deeper meaning to these small elements of our lives. These elements continue to dog us with their repeated voices that cry out for our attention though unheeded by us.

Maybe by yielding attention to these seemingly small needs that present themselves we'll find ourselves in tune with other nuances of life about us. Maybe by yielding our attention on a regular moment-by-moment basis, we'll notice things we've missed in the past. Maybe we'll find ourselves more in tune with the elements and creatures who share our environment. And on the level of the minuscule, we may find lost parts of ourselves.

The only requirement on our part is to pause and give our attention to the moment, and 'listen' to whatever voice might be speaking. The response required of us might be simpler than we think...even a slight turn of a screw.

Boundaries

The snow has melted, we've had some rain, and as we drive through the countryside we take notice of the varying shades of browns and greens divided by unbelievably straight lines and fences, separating field from field and property from property.

Boundary lines help us and our neighbors define where our property ends and theirs begins. They define our space as well. While some of us recognize our space and the importance of guarding it, others may not have any understanding of that personal space and disregard it totally. But we all have need of space that we can call our own; tangible and intangible space. I remember when I was quite young, spending the weekend with a friend in her home. She announced to me before we went to bed that she didn't wish to talk in the morning until after her coffee. I appreciated that fact that she defined her wishes so clearly. I was a sunny talkative morning person and could easily have violated her boundaries unknowingly. I've thought many times since, how good it was that she so clearly defined her boundaries, and how much I learned from that one experience.

But not everyone has that candor. The trouble with many of us is that we don't define our boundaries, and when someone violates those undefined boundaries we experience resentment, frustration, anger and confusion.

Defining boundaries was an issue in the movie 'Never Cry Wolf.' The man who was out in the wilds among the wolves watched to see how the wolves declared their boundaries and himself followed suit. They were then able to live together, yet separate, understanding and recognizing each others boundaries. Boundaries help to keep us from building walls of misunderstanding.

Boundaries can be beautiful. They're helpful in the fields. They're helpful in our lives. We need to be sensitive to ours and other's boundaries in order to keep lines of communication open.

A Few Thoughts on Time

et's suppose that everyone in the whole wide world were rationed an equal amount of money on a regular daily basis. No one would be allowed, under this law, to beg, borrow, steal or accumulate more money than each individual had been given. Let's suppose, also, that this law left people with no choice but to obey it because it just could not, physically, be broken.

This stipulated amount of rationed money would be adequate to cover each individual's needs, plus a little extra for secondary needs like fun, recreation and creativity. This sounds fair, does it not? That is unless a person wouldn't be satisfied with merely having their needs met, having a desire to accumulate—or wanting more fun and recreation than the rationed amount would allow.

No doubt such an idea as this has been chewed and hashed over numerous times down through the years by people with better understanding of economics than I might possess.

However, this analogy is not designed to be a study in economics, but to help us look at our allotted time in a new and different perspective. Time might be looked upon as a commodity that is very precious to each one of us. Precious, because it's so easily lost, mis-spent or killed in one way or another.

Time must be carefully guarded lest we spend it on less important things and have none left for the things we value the most.

For most of us, nowadays, the desire for more time becomes acute; and some of us talk and think about time the way that a starving person might think and talk about food.

"If only I had more time..." is the cry. But how wisely do we use that precious time that's been allotted to us? How discerning are we when it comes to those hours of free time, especially?

Time has unlimited value, and if it could be purchased as a commodity, it would no doubt, be of greater value than gold.

With this most precious allotment of time that each of us has been given, on a regular daily basis, let's be careful how we use it. Let us remember not to spend it too far ahead and find ourselves with a time deficit. Let us spend it with care and guard it well. Let us, also, remember that it can be used as a gift. To give another the precious gift of our time—can be what that soul might need the very most.

I Think, Therefore;
I Make My Own Decisions

As I sit in the coolness and warmth of a sunny morning on my beloved front porch, I find that I'm torn between work and rest. As my neighbors mow their lawns, I'm made conscious of the fact that my lawn also needs mowing. Guilt begins to creep in, saying; you should be mowing your lawn. Then perfect rest and relaxation become impossible. Continuing to enjoy the atmosphere of my porch will cost me a tight knot of anxiety in my stomach. I can no longer just 'Be'—I must 'Do' in order to relieve the pressure.

Living in a neighborhood, rather than out in a remote spot in the country, makes one more conscious of this conflict between Being and Doing, especially in the summer when one becomes more conscious of what the neighbors are doing. There seems to be a collective-consciousness in a neighborhood that dictates, to some degree, when it's time to do this or that outdoor chore. But being a rebel at heart, I don't like to be dictated to. My desire is to move with the rhythm of inspiration and/or intuition, i.e. "There-is-a-time-for-everything-under-the-sun…" sort of thinking. And yet, I admit and confess that collective-consciousness interferes with my own natural rhythms. To what degree, I cannot tell.

I speak of the collective consciousness in terms of the most tangible evidence—trends! Like, today is the day when all able-bodied people in our neighborhood get out and mow their lawns. But there are also many other trends that are somewhat less obvious. Trends that move like an ocean wave in a certain direction carrying with it everything that isn't anchored.

Styles in clothes are one of those trends. They come and they go. And when they're gone, one is stuck with perfectly good, wearable clothes that are no longer in style. But if one doesn't keep up with the styles—isn't savvy about what's in and what's not—one may show up at an important convention wearing a cotton dress (a beautiful cotton dress I might add) while every other living soul at the convention is wearing the newest fashion—polyester suits!! And that's exactly what I did many, many years ago. Did I feel uncomfortable and out of place? Indeed I did! I searched in vain for one other individual who was not sporting polyester…but found not one!

But that was then and this is now. I want to believe that the person I am today could have more gracefully accepted that which made me appear so different. I think…I hope…that I've become more of an individual since then, more comfortable with who I am.

Now, bell-bottom trousers are returning. Those nostalgic people who tucked such trousers into boxes to store in the attic feel some degree of triumph that they're in possession of a 'vintage' pair (even though they may have shrunk in the attic). And so it goes…trends and styles.

However, my greatest interest is not in the realm of the collective-conscious, where we are aware to some degree that we're 'buying into' a trend. My fascination lies with the realm of the collective-unconscious; that which is so subliminal that we have no idea we're being influenced. We may even believe that we are experiencing an original thought, only to learn later that many others have experienced that same 'original' thought.

Whether it is the collective-consciousness or the collective-unconsciousness that has the power to influence, are we not left with a choice in the matter? It is for each individual to think and decide whether what one does is out of the very core of one's being—one's own true path—or out of the easy path of allowing others to do our thinking for us.

I see a metaphor for this kind of mentality in the way we've bought into the Quick-fix and fast-food ideas that says, "Tell me what to do and I'll do it"—or "You make it for me and I'll eat it!"

James Hillman speaks of our own unique and individual destiny in his recent book, The Soul's Code. He speaks of the acorn theory—one that Aristotle developed several centuries ago. The essence of the oak tree lies within the acorn. Whether we plant that acorn in the sterile, sandy soil of blind-obedience to the trends or waves of the age in which we live, or in the rich fertile soil of inspiration, imagination and reflection, will determine the fullness of destiny that lies in our acorn.

There is a degree of risk involved when we follow our own path, rather than go-with-the-flow. One must budget mistakes into the bargain. There is no guarantee that we will not fall into error. There is before us the safe path, the well-trodden path of herd instinct, conformity to trends and current thought. And there is also the path of adventure in the unknown and uncertain future. This is the path that affirms our own true identity, as we act upon the intuition that comes to us from the very heart of our being. This path may come to us with a high price, maybe, but wouldn't it be well worth it to make the journey?

And now, as the drone of the lawnmowers surrounds me, after enjoying a pleasant morning on the front porch, as I philosophize about my 'duty' to myself and my neighbors, the knot in my stomach has relaxed and I've shed the burden of guilt. At this point in time, I think I'll mow my lawn.

Stirring Dull Roots

"The winter is past...The Flowers appear on earth, the time for singing of birds is come, and the voice of the turtle is heard in the land."

Spring seems so much more like a New Beginning than January 1st. Spring—a time for Resurrection of all that has lain dormant throughout the long, cold winter. And with that resurrection of the leaves out of bare branches, tulips out of barren ground and bird song filling the air—comes a resurrection of heart.

There is new hope, fresh ideas, joy and gladness of heart;

Lilacs out of dead land, mixing memory and desire, stirring dull roots with spring rain.

What a wonderful opportunity for change, for following one's bliss, for breaking out of old, dull patterns of living and thinking.

What is it that I've wanted to do? What changes have I desired to make? What transformations have I been dreaming of undergoing?

What holds me back? Hopefully, not old habits and patterns that keep me stuck in a hopeless rut.

In one of my most recent and ancient books I've been reading, I read of a boy whose spring ritual was to make a grand and wonderful kite. He made it; he didn't buy it. He painted a dragon on it, and made the tail of the kite to look like the dragon's tail, and then he brought some very strong string and let his kite soar into the sky. To the boy, it was symbolic of his own spirit soaring high in the sky while he made the flight of the kite possible by tethering it to the earth. The boy and the kite were one. It brought me such joy to read this story that it made me want to make a grand kite, myself, this spring. I hope that old habits and patterns don't stand in my way. If you see a wonderful grand kite in the color of lilac soaring high above the city of St. Cloud, you'll know who it belongs to.

The Softening Effect

few months ago I was invited to a meeting in one of the rooms at our local library. I was impressed with the warmth and hospitality of the group and the discussion. But what impressed me the most was the fact that one of the people, Betty, had brought items from home to adorn the tables. There were several green plants artfully placed on the functional tables that are typical of a public place. There were hand-woven rugs on the tables on which the plants were placed. There was a wicker stool on which a lovely piece of cloth was casually draped.

As Betty dismantled the tables that had been, for a brief time, so beautiful, I spoke with her. I expressed my appreciation for what she had done to bring warmth and beauty to an otherwise functional environment. "It helps soften things," she said, as she carefully packed all of her treasures and beautiful props into boxes to take home again.

The thought of 'softening things' has remained with me, ever since, and I've followed her example whenever possible in public places with simple things like green plants and woven rugs and wicker stools draped with lovely cloth.

I am reminded of a time several years ago when I returned home at the end of a long and busy day to find a candle-lit table, and a carefully and lovingly prepared dinner waiting for me. There were fresh flowers on the table and cloth napkins artfully folded. There was music playing. The dinner was delicious, although I cannot remember what was served. But the memory of the setting for that dinner definitely lives on.

Since that time I have, as much as possible, placed candles on the dinner table and flowers and cloth napkins, because in that moment of time, when I arrived home and beheld the beautiful scene, I realized the value of such touches. They soften things.

In the barrenness of busyness our souls starve for some thoughtful adornments. We need these places, these little retreats, even if it be only for an hour. A time that allows one to sink back into one's chair and into the experience of the moment and enjoy the atmosphere…allowing one to return to the duties and obligations of life, more rested and refreshed, in remembrance of the beauty.

As we move into this busiest time of the year, it might help if we pause, every-so-often to look around us and find places that we can soften for those who may be very much in need of the softening effect of beauty and comfort, and thought-full-ness.

A Chance to Dance

ven though I am not an antique car buff, I had noticed the neat little number sitting outside the Co-op one day. It was a white Volkswagen Bug that looked in mint condition with not a spot or wrinkle anywhere in sight. It was decorated with a sleek green stripe with a few curly-cues. It had unique, shiny hub caps, and the picture I saw made an impression on me that brought a smile.

Shortly thereafter, a young man in his middle teens peddling a dirt bike came down the sidewalk. He saw the Bug and became so enthralled with the sight he almost ran into it, made a quick maneuver avoiding a collision. First he sat on his bike and stared. Then he laid his bike on the sidewalk and began half circling the little vehicle. Back and forth he went. His body language, I thought, was almost a dance as I watched the various movements. He went to the front part and sat on his haunches, hands on his upper legs. He got up and spread out his arms—hands lifted, palms upward. He'd start toward his bike to leave, then turn around and go back to his former movements—up, down, around, back and forth. He tried to pull himself away several times, going back to his bike, picking it up, then laying it down again to return to that which so captivated his attention. And then, he was finally on his bike and gone.

For my part, I was captivated by his antics. It was pure delight to watch him. He was poetry in motion. The dance has ended, but the memory remains. I, in my imagination, go back to my place of watcher. The scene has imprinted itself in my heart.

Why, I asked myself, was I so enthralled? Because of the genuine, unabashed enthusiasm and passion that I beheld in observing this young 'lover' held captive in a moment of time by a thing of beauty to which the young man paid tribute.

The world for many has become so mundane...so tragically busy...so complicated. There is little room for enthusiasm, joy, delight, spontaneity, and we often miss the dance because we weren't even aware of the music...the beauty...the splendor of life.

Whether one dances around a fascinating little car or with one's children, mate, or grandchildren, it matters not. What matters most is our readiness to dance when the next opportunity presents itself.

The Price of Progress

everal months ago a book came into my hands that caused me to see things from a perspective I'd never previously experienced. The book, <u>Night Flying Woman</u>, told the story of an Ojibwa Indian woman living in the nineteenth century; written by a great-granddaughter, Ignatia Broker.

Although the account focused on one woman, it told the story of the Ojibwas of Northern Minnesota and Dakota, quite vividly. It told of their daily lives, how they gathered their food, how they lived, their relationships to each other within their tribe, and what they believed.

Their lives were lived in relationship to the Earth, its yield, and its changing seasons. It also told of the great respect they had for the elders who carried the memories and history of their people. Their respect and appreciation of the land and of the elders revealed a reverence for their roots and traditions. I strongly sensed that their way of life was far more nourishing to the individual spirit than anything I'd experienced in my own culture.

As the story of this woman and her family unfolded, the author revealed how the white people and their ways began to infringe up on the lives of these Native Americans, as the white people gradually moved in and eventually took over. It seemed, as I read, as if a disease had begun to spread and kill off the vegetation and forests of the Northern Minnesota and Dakota. The Ojibwa people were driven deeper and deeper into the forests until there was little of forest left in which to seek refuge.

When the Natives finally encountered the Intruder, their lives took a surprising twist. The Whites possessed things that tempted the Native People. These items were such things as glass fruit jars, iron kettles, calico cloth and lumber. The lumber, of course, would build more permanent dwellings for the Natives. However, in order for the Natives to obtain these' treasures' they would need to have the white people's money. In order to obtain this medium of exchange they would not only work for the White people, but learn to adapt to the White's way of life. One requirement was sending their children to boarding schools, thereby separating child from family for months at a time. The father, also, had to leave the home and go off to work for the Whites. The Ojibwa families became split.

As the story of the Night Flying Woman unfolded, I reflected, sadly, on how much these Native peoples were losing of their own culture and identity in their pursuit of what the White people's technology had to offer. Once begun, there was no turning back. This was, of course, looked upon as 'progress'.

Glass fruit jars, iron pots, calico cloth, and lumber, no doubt, offered a better way of life, a higher standard of living for these Native Americans. But one cannot help but wonder how much quality of life was sacrificed. What a high price they paid! What great loss of family and both personal and cultural identity.

And yet, isn't this story reminiscent of our own story? Do we stop to ask what we might be sacrificing as we seek to raise our own standard of living? Do we consider whether we might be losing quality of life in pursuit of some better, new, improved technology? Do we ask whether we'll be brought closer to friends and family, or more isolated by the choices we make? How much do we really count the cost?

Freedom to Choose

he month of July makes us recall Independence Day, and we, in our various ways, celebrate Independence that was won as the new Americans severed themselves from the British empire. How much that Independence means to each person cannot be measured by statistics.

Living in a free country, most of us don't know what freedom means. One only knows what Freedom means when it has been withheld...then one longs for freedom from insignificance...oppression...dictatorship.

A person who has lived under the power of a person or state or regimen of some sort will more readily define 'freedom' because that person thinks about it and longs for it, thereby becoming more familiar with the term. A person who already has freedom tends to take it for granted and rarely thinks about it.

So what does freedom mean to you? Are we more familiar with freedom-from or freedom to? Freedom-from denotes a release of a sort. Freedom-to denotes a recognition of the rights that belong to us, requiring an action on our part to possess that freedom fully.

This raises the question:"What am I free to do?"Am I free to be me? Or do I concern myself with what others will think of me if I express myself in a certain way. Do I allow others to make my decisions by *remote control?*' When I ask, "What will people think?" sets limits on our behavior, who I am, how I conduct myself in this world. What matters most is what *I* think about what I do. When I become conscious of my own personal freedom, I sometimes become an irritant to others. I won't just 'go-with-the-flow' when I recognize my right to choose. And I won't yield to others the power that I've been given, through personal choice.

However, to defer to a person who is depleted of their own power of choice can be a valuable gift. These people are sometimes children, sometimes aged, sometimes minorities, and sometimes the infirm.

Those who already have more power than they need are the politicians and professionals. They are the wealthy and the very well-learned. We allow such people to decide for us about our lives because we're uncertain of our own abilities to make the right choices. We abdicate to others the responsibility that belongs to us as individuals. But these people are not to be blamed for our inability to boldly make our own choices. We, as individuals, need to recognize our individual gifts of insight and recognize that our own considered opinion is valuable to the whole.

Celebrating the Independence that results in our unique individuality ultimately leads to our ability to cooperate. This article is not intended to address any current moral, social, or political issue. The only intention is to increase awareness of the responsibility incumbent upon us to Think, to Choose, to Decide, and to Act.

A Way of Seeing

here was a time, long, long ago when people didn't have labor-saving devices, such as automatic washers, dryers, dishwashers, cars, computers, vending machines, and all of those things designed to make the life of a human being more convenient as well as time-saving.

Life was simpler before all of these conveniences. There wasn't as much garbage, either. We didn't have to worry about making enough money to keep us supplied with all these conveniences.

Back in those days, human beings were more in touch with nature—more aware of the origin of things. Everyone knew where milk originated, where the grains for our cereal and bread came from, how vegetables were grown, where meat and wool and cloth and other materials originated.

Nowadays, almost everything comes to us in a package and we've lost connection with our source of supply. Some children are actually astonished to find how milk comes from a cow or a goat. They thought it was, somehow, manufactured—and it was, but not the way they thought.

With that loss of connection from our source, we've also lost a very important part of ourselves. The organic part of us—that part that once lived in harmony with nature that part of us that could commune with nature around us—the trees, the birds, the land—its gentle slopes and hills—the patch work of colors that our organic eyes remain hungry for—and our soul desires to absorb into itself.

We've made ourselves strangers to our environment. We've alienated ourselves from the very source of joy and happiness that are to be found in organic life, in exchange for concrete, steel, and electricity.

Some of these things—technologies, conveniences—are hard to give up, even if the desire to live a simpler life is there. But what we can do, as we seek to 'vacate,' to 'recreate,' is to find a place that offers us an opportunity to reacquaint ourselves with the wonder of nature round about us.

Let's try to re-discover some of the things that brought us a sense of awe and wonder as children. Let's make a journey back to our roots. Let's seek the peace and contentment that can come to us when we slow down and take notice of the beauty of creation. We might find, in our re-discovery of the abundant beauty that nature has to offer us that we don't 'need' so much in the way of artificial stimulation as we thought we did.

In Search of Ponies

he story goes that a scientific experiment was being performed where two little boys were involved. One boy was placed in a room full of every imaginable and unique toy, and the other was placed in a room full of horse manure and a shovel. The doors were shut on them, and they were each left to their own devices.

An hour later, the scientists came back for a progress check. The first little boy was bored with the toys, and many of them lay broken. He wasn't happy. When they checked on the second little boy, they say that he was smiling, whistling, and shoveling the horse manure. Puzzled at his delight, the scientist asked him why he was so happy as he shoveled away. His enthusiastic reply was, "With all this horse manure, I thought there must be a pony in here somewhere."

Friends with whom I've shared this little story will often remind one another, when hard times confront us, "there must be a pony in here somewhere."

At times such as these, when the whole world appears to us to be a roomful of that pungent mess, we need to look for meaning and purpose in it all.

A quotation from the diary of Etty Hillesun (a young Jewish woman in Holland during the holocaust of World War II), "We need to reclaim large areas of peace in ourselves, more and more peace, and reflect it to others—and the more peace there is in us, the more peace there will be in our troubled world. That," Etty said, "is our moral duty."*

Our attitude toward life, people, events in our lives and in the world, has a direct effect on others around us, either positive or negative. It's good for our health and the health of our immediate environment as well as the health of the

* An Interrupted Live

54

world in which we live to "reclaim large areas of peace in our own lives..." As difficult as this may seem at times, the value of such a pursuit cannot be measured. We can make a difference when this becomes our response—our contribution, if you will—toward world peace.

Given the fact that people have varying views on world events, we need to listen deeply to one another with respect and courtesy—not fearing to hear the other side. That way, we can encourage peace with one another on an individual basis, hopefully, creating a ripple effect. We also may learn something by listening.

Therein is it possible...we may find that pony?

Matters of the Heart

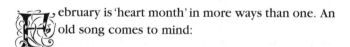ebruary is 'heart month' in more ways than one. An old song comes to mind:

> Ya' gotta have heart,
>
> All ya' really need is heart.
>
> When the odds are sayin'
>
> You'll never win
>
> That's when the grin should start...

Heart in the sense that that song depicts is a kind of fortitude of spirit that rises up from the center of one's being when adversity strikes. "When the odds are sayin' you'll never win—" the heroic heart breaks forth as rays of sun through dark clouds.

Adversity brings great opportunity for the heroic spirit to reveal itself as we draw on these hidden resources within ourselves—the David within us meeting the Goliath of threat.

We're happier with ourselves and our performance when misfortune strikes, when adversity strikes and we meet it with a courageous heart, we begin to live life on a different plane for a few hours, days, weeks, or months! The good consequence of such misfortune is that it gives us opportunity to be drawn closer together—heart to heart—shoulder to shoulder with a common goal, a common purpose.

Those who aren't willing to confront the challenge of crisis, burying their heads in sand, are left behind to face the dreariness of a life not lived to its fullest.

Movies, such as "Dances with Wolves," "Grand Canyon," "Black Hawk Down," "Strangers in Good Company," and "Man from Snowy River" (among many others) draw us because there's that element in such movies that depict stories of risk, adventure, daring, revealed through the heroes and heroines of such stories. Our hearts are deeply touched and resonate.

We face the possibility of adversity that recession or depression might bring. We face illnesses that are coming upon us as a result of depleted ozone, acid rain, contaminated ground water, air pollution, as well as chemicals and pesticides in our food.

Times like this will bring out the worst or the best in us. There's a new frontier to conquer. And we need to remind ourselves that we have the resources within to meet the challenge of this age if we 'take heart.'

And yet we really don't want any misfortune to come upon us—and we certainly don't welcome it when it comes. We would not be sane if we had such an attitude. We prefer the daily routine of predictability over the uncertain adventure that such calamities bring.

As I continue, with rapt interest, to re-read Laura Ingalls Wilder's <u>Little House on the Prairie</u> series, I'm so struck by the love and concern exhibited within the family and without— to friends and neighbors who endure equal hardships. There was often the risk of life and limb to help others, and there comes a resulting unbreakable bond as Heart meets Heart.

Unwanted Growth

I have a tree—a very large tree—growing in the small space between my garage and wooden fence. I didn't intend for it to be there, I didn't plan it. Yet I didn't stop it either when I saw the flourishing branches. Somehow, without giving it much thought, I just left it alone. Now it shades a very large portion of my backyard, for good and for bad.

I also have a tree that *pretends* it's a vine growing along the side of my house, next to the foundation. When I realized it was getting out of hand, I went after it with pruning shears and cut back all the branches, not doing anything to the root system. It only became stronger as a result of the pruning. It now shades my living room window and has begun to give shade to the second story window of my bedroom as well. I'm glad the foundation of my house is made of granite; I think, I hope, the granite will be able to withstand the root system. That is, no doubt, as healthy as the part above the ground.

Both trees were, for me, unwanted growth that I've come to terms with. Maybe it's okay that they are where they are, maybe it's a good thing that the seeds took root and grew into these healthy trees…I think….

Since I would not dream of growing a tree from a seed rather than a sapling, I hadn't dreamed of a little seed sprouting such a large tree. Since I now realize the power of a small seed I'm more careful to nip all those little new sprouts in the early stages and put a stop to their continued growth.

What has given me more food for thought on the subject of unwanted growth is how I may allow an opinion, a bias, a prejudiced statement of a friend, colleague or stranger to be dropped, like a seed, into my mind and allow it to germinate there until it begins to develop a root-system that's hard to get rid of. The question arises: am I going to challenge or confront that thought or idea? Do I agree or disagree? Or do I just not give it much thought and consideration as to whether I want or don't want that idea to take root in my thinking processes?

Something I've become conscious of lately in our community is a growing prejudice towards newcomers. I hear snatches of conversation on the Metro Bus that takes me to and from The Good Earth. One conversation between bus driver and passenger, and their blatant hostility toward the newcomers required me to call the Metro Bus office and report what I heard to someone in authority. Was I too chicken to confront driver and the passenger? I don't know. Let the reader decide.

Something else that happened recently had to do with an article in the St. Cloud Times. The reputation of an individual—actually one of our co-op customers—was placed in jeopardy in an article the Times carried. I was shocked and dismayed. Was it true? I didn't know. But something that was very clear to me as I read the article was that the whole story wasn't there. It was one sided— that was plain to see. But without hearing the whole story, what can one conclude? Can one make a judgment based on a one sided story?

I thought of something that I came to realize several years ago, i.e., if a police car were to pull up in front of my house and the police were to lead one of us away in handcuffs, would my neighbors say "I wonder what he/she did?" or would they say "I wonder if he/she did anything?" I wondered too what *I'd* think if that were to happen to a neighbor. Would I remember to withhold judgment in light of the fact that I didn't know the whole story? Or would I automatically form an opinion based on the evidence I had?

It is a difficult but worthy task to watch for those little sprouts of growth that so quickly develop as a result of someone's idea, opinion, or story being dropped into our minds. We need clarity. We need to be watchful. We need to be conscious of whether we're allowing unwanted growth that could do damage to the structure of ours and others lives.

If there's any one thing in my study of Dr. Carl Jung and his works and philosophy that has helped me the most, it is learning that the world's evil lies not only outside of me, but within me. If I can but remember that, I can shed the 'us against them' attitude that is such a hindrance to personal and world peace, but so ingrained in the human condition.

Our obligation to ourselves and our fellow human beings lies in being more and more conscious of the various ways in which we may be allowing undesirable, unwanted seeds of prejudice to take root in our individual spheres of life.

There's a Time for Everything...
A Time to Look Beneath the Surface

ne of the greatest lessons I've learned in the process of living this life of mine is; "If you want to make any improvement, things always have to get worse before they get better."

A most common metaphor in life is improving one's home through redecoration or remodeling. One just cannot improve the situation without causing a great mess! One of the situations that arose to teach me this very great truth took place about 25 years ago when our family returned to Minnesota after living six and a half years in Southern California. We sought an older home and found one. It was in a desirable location and a graceful old home, although greatly in need of sprucing up.

The first job I tackled the following spring was an upstairs bedroom. I decided upon a quick-fix by painting over the existing wallpaper and be all finished by the end of the day. Two weeks later, with aching muscles, we were still not done, although I'd involved other members of the family in this simple task. We were slowly steaming off the old wallpaper that had begun to pucker and loosen as wet paint was applied. Beneath the wallpaper was crumbling plaster that loosened from the shiplap. As more and more of the crumbling plaster came off with the wallpaper I realized this was a much bigger job than I'd anticipated when I began my efforts.

My hope of a quick fix had long since crumbled along with stubborn wallpaper and crumbling plaster, with no end in sight. I had not anticipated the problems I'd uncovered behind the smooth facades of wallpaper. It was at the point of despair and uncertainty that the truth came home to me: Things always have to get worse before they get better. In spite of my weary body and aching muscles, a wry smile passed over my face as I realized what a great metaphorical truth I was learning. I have not forgotten it since and have had many occasions to quote this great truth to others, lest we have the experience but miss the meaning.

Life, real life is incredibly messy! We find this to be true when we can no longer accept the status quo; the chronic condition and we desire or need to move toward change, improvement, resolution. It's not only messy, but scary! We don't know what lies behind the facades, behind the illusion of the security of sameness. So why not just leave things as they are? Why not leave well enough alone? Avoid the mess and continue to live with the familiar, the predictable. Why not? Maybe because new life is breaking through the surface of one's very being, just as new life begins to break through the ground in the spring, and can't be held back; we must allow it to burst forth. Our part of the spring ritual is to help it along. We rake away the dead leaves. We loosen the ground around the new life, and in the process we let ourselves get messy, for a time, as we offer aid to that which promises potential and beauty, out of the luxurious new growth.

However, if one wishes to avoid the mess of change and growth, one may choose the status quo rather than finding what lies beneath the surface and all the work involved. One might choose to live with the security of sameness, of predictability of control of our situation, rather than delve beneath the surface and face the unknown possibilities. But—is that really living?

Beginning the New Year as a "Beginner"

ometimes Heroism and Integrity pop up in the most unusual places and in most astonishing ways. An example of this is contained in the following story.

One Saturday afternoon I was sitting in the front seat of one of our metro buses. When I boarded the bus I noticed four or five adolescent boys were occupying some of the rear seats. I couldn't help but notice during our trip downtown the usual banter one comes to expect from boys of that age. However, there was nothing unruly or overly loud or disturbing in their chatter and banter to interfere with reading my book.

As we neared the bus terminal, a group of college age men were standing on the corner of 5th Avenue talking amongst themselves. One of the young men stood out from the others. His head was shaved except for a strip of hair down the middle of his head from the forehead to the neck. That strip had been colored and then molded into half a dozen or so spikes that were made stiff by some sort of goo that made them straight out from his head. His appearance definitely drew my attention.

The attention of the boys in the rear seat was also drawn to the young man, and various uncomplimentary descriptive words began to tumble out of their mouths along with a bit of jeering and some epithets mixed in.

I wasn't surprised at their reaction, but what I hadn't expected was a very loud outburst from one of the boys: 'Shut up!' And they all, surprisingly, quickly shut up. Dead silence followed for the remainder of our trip, quite an amazing turn from the flowing talk and banter that had existed only a few moments earlier.

My heart was stirred by the heroism of the boy who wasn't afraid to speak his own truth in the face of the majority. I was also aware of the respect shown by his peers in their utter silence. Not one little challenge, not one peep from any of those who'd been so brash and boisterous a few moments earlier. No doubt they, like me, were in a state of shock. But it was a good kind of shock. I wish we could be 'shocked' like that more often.

That simple act, that one, lone, clear voice lingers in my memory. Such courage he displayed in the face of group pressure. I couldn't help but wonder what had gone into his own young life story that generated an exhibition of such spirit!

But the story continues. When I got downtown I had a close view of the young man with the spiked hair. I saw his face. It bore a gentle expression, almost angelic. Such a great contrast to the punk hair! Surprised by the contrast, I asked myself, "What did you expect?"

The entire experience was more than I could decipher at the moment. Some things however, can never be fully deciphered, but all can still receive the 'message' at the deeper level where meaning unfolds. Lest we have the experience but miss the meaning, let us be more willing to open our hearts to the inexplicable, mysterious things that happen to us, act upon us, and around us, as we enter this New Year. It might be that "The Beginner's Mind" we open new doors of perception to this world in which we find ourselves.

A Birthday "Wish"

inding myself in a celebratory spirit as I enter my 65th year on earth, I want to extend to you a birthday wish…from me to you! I saw the movie Bridges of Madison County this past year, and it touched me deeply. Then I read the book, and it touched me more deeply still. Because of my love affair with the story, a friend gave me the video for Christmas. I saw the story, again, the first week in January, and was moved greatly by the introduction in the letter that Francesca had written to her children. It was to be read at the time of her death. "I could let this die with me, I suppose, but as one grows older one's fears subside. What becomes more and more important is to be known, known for all that you were during this brief stay. How sad it seems to me to leave this earth without those you love the most ever really knowing who you were."

My "wish" is to know you and to be known by you—it is of prime importance to me. I've endeavored to know myself as much as possible, and now, I ask that you allow me to be myself as much as possible in your presence. I invite you to be yourself in my presence that I may grow to know you better.

Knowing one another is an illusive, dynamic activity because if we are growing and/or evolving, we're in a continual flux. Those close to us don't always welcome the changes that unfold. I realized, last summer, how resistant I am to change when my granddaughter, Stephanie's preferences in food and clothing radically altered. Instead of frilly, twirly dresses and skirts, she wanted jeans. Instead of grandma's wholesome soups, sandwiches, and salads she preferred Spaghetti-O's and MacDonald's Happy Meals. One afternoon I became frustrated at my inability to satisfy her choices of food and dress. Bordering on tears I said, "I don't know what you want anymore! You don't like the clothes I offer you, you don't like my food anymore...I don't know what to do."

I barely finished my litany of complaints when she burst into tears with the response, "I don't know either. I don't know what happened to that little girl who liked your vegetable soup and pasta salad and dresses. Grandma, I don't know what happened to her!"

My heart melted at that tumble of words, as I realized that her dilemma was greater than mine. I gave her a long hug and begged her forgiveness, and began accepting her changes. In Bridges of Madison County, Francesca's grown children wanted to reject the contents of her letter. There had been great resistance to knowing their mother as she was requiring them to know her. Yet, as the story unfolded, 'hearing' her out generated profound changes in them. They were forced into a new phase of understanding, first their mother, and then themselves. Their resulting acceptance of who their mother truly was, set them free to take a new look at themselves in light of their changed perspectives regarding 'Mom.'

Like Francesca's children and Stephanie's Grandma, there is a resistance in allowing others to live our own truth. When that resistance is too threatening, we pull others, including ourselves, back like hermit crabs, into our shell, fearful of being wounded beyond what we can endure.

But wouldn't it be wonderful if we could be known for all that we are during "this brief stay on earth" and find acceptance from those we love?

Meeting Our Basic Needs

everal years ago I was sitting on a bench at the Crossroads waiting to meet a friend. The scene that unfolded before me is as clear now as it was then. There was a mother and a child who was crying hard and loud. The mother was hurrying toward a nutrition shop where she and the baby disappeared for a few moments. When they emerged again, the mother brought the baby over to the area where I was sitting. She put her crying baby in its stroller and hurriedly opened a container of yogurt she'd purchased.

I sat in rapt fascination and wonderment. Did this young mother find the solution to the immediate problem of her child? I watched expectantly as she dipped the plastic spoon into the yogurt container and offered it to her sobbing baby. Open went the little mouth, down went the yogurt, along with a few little baby sounds that often occur at feeding time. The sobbing was alleviated as another spoonful of yogurt was received with relish. Spoonful after spoonful of yogurt went into the little mouth, while the sobbing had completely ceased. The sounds of satisfied "mmms" continued. The mother's wisdom in the matter of her baby's needs proved accurate, and it made me happy as I observed the entire scene.

After the primal needs were met, the little eyes began to rove over to the environment of which I was a part. The eyes came to rest on me, and I responded with a smile. Instinctively, the child's hand reached out to touch mother's leg. Another spoonful of yogurt, another glance toward the stranger who smiled, and it wasn't long before the child could lean back, in a relaxed fashion in the stroller, and smile back at the stranger. But the big toe needed to touch the mother's leg...just the toe!

The image of that mother and child has come back to me over and over through the years. Why? Maybe because of the delight I felt along with the child, in having a need met by someone who loves, someone who might know what is needed, even if the one in need doesn't.

We all have those needs, as the little child so graphically illustrates in this story. Yet, we as adults have learned to control ourselves; we've learned to contain our emotions. And we've even learned to practice denial of our basic needs. As a result of learning to negate ourselves, in not allowing others to know that we are hurting, that we need help, the emotional pain lodges somewhere in our body, and manifests itself on another level be it a physical ailment or a mental disorder. The need becomes buried deep in our flesh and bones, and we think we can remedy the need in some other way, by some other means. But the need will remain. While the symptoms might be treated, the pain alleviated, the need still must be honored and must be met. But how?

Some experiences of our own childhood may hold the key. Going back into our own individual stories, in a sense reliving our stories in a way that can cause us to observe as I observed the scene of mother and child at the Crossroads, a time when we were crying out in need, but no one was there for us. Or else, someone was there and told us to stop crying without meeting the need. We've all had those times, some worse than others, when something that needed to be done wasn't done for us. And so we continue to carry the pain of it, the memory and source of pain long forgotten. We need to relive and honor those memories, and give comfort to that little child in us, in the same way we would reach out as adults to a child we see in need, offering nourishment and comfort. We also need to do that for the child in one another.

Having our needs met frees us up to explore the world around us, as we remain in touch with the source of comfort…touching that source, if only with one little toe!!!

The Sound of Roses

We've suffered through a long and very cold winter. And now we begin to apprehend the possibility of Spring, of new life springing up out of the long frozen ground, and green buds swelling into leaf on bare branches. As the season turns from frigid to warm, and fallow ground bursts forth with the first signs of spring; pussywillows, violets, crocuses, cowslips, tulips, and lilies, I always feel some pangs of pain in this particular change of season that brings with it such great beauty.

In this state of nostalgia, memories of past springs parade through my thoughts. Some memories are bittersweet, memories of my beloved son, Les, who died of cancer four years ago in April. As the last hours of his life began to unfold, those hours we didn't know were his last, and the pain became unrelenting. With a twinkle in his eye, he called that particular day, "share the pain day." The day was Good Friday. The following day he quietly slipped out of his cloak of flesh and left this realm.

There was great peace in those hours.

The weather, which had been cold and dreary and rainy, changed radically the next day. The sun burst forth in its entire splendor, and it became so warm that Easter morning I was able to open wide the doors and windows. We didn't need coats or jackets. Later in the day, the weather returned to its cold, rainy dreariness again. I will always remember that spring…and its distinctive days.

We had invited several people who represented various aspects of Les's life to speak. As we who were closest to Les listened to their stories we realized that none of us had fully known this person. Les didn't talk much about himself or what he did. He had quietly worked behind the scenes facilitating, helping others, ever so quietly, so that even I, his mother, had not known this person as I fully came to know him in the telling of those stories from various perspectives.

One of his friends, Mark, who shared his passion for audio recording, spoke of Les's love of the sounds of nature and always bringing his recording equipment to the North Shore of Lake Superior and setting it up on sand and gravel to capture and bring back the sounds of water splashing over the rocks, the sand, the gravel…and all of the various subtle sounds of nature. Mark said, in closing, Les would tell you if he were here, "Stop, and listen to the roses."

Since that point of time in my life, a door of perception opened wider for me. A door of awareness. A door that opens in one's heart to see and hear and celebrate the beauty Nature has to offer. A door that intensifies my ability to smell, to see, to touch, to taste, to hear…(to listen).

As spring approaches…the long awaited Spring!…be ready…to experience…the Joy!!!

Thoughts Reminiscent of The Rubaiyat of Omar Khayam

A Book of Verses underneath the Bough

A Jug of Wine, a Loaf of Bread—and Thou

Beside me singing in the Wilderness—

Oh, Wilderness were Paradise Enow!

There here was a time, long long ago when people didn't have labor-saving devices, such as automatic washers, dryers, dishwashers, and all of those things designed to make the life of a human being more convenient as well as time-saving.

Life was simpler before all of these conveniences. There wasn't as much garbage, either. We didn't have to worry about making enough money to keep us supplied with all these conveniences.

Back in those days, human beings were more in touch with nature—more aware of the origin of things. Everyone knew where milk originated, where the grains for our cereal and bread came from, how vegetables were grown, where meat and wool and cloth and other materials originated.

Nowadays, everything comes to us in a package, almost, and we've lost connection with our source of supply. Some children are actually astonished to find that milk comes from a cow or a goat. They thought it was, somehow, manufactured—and it was, but not the way they thought.

With that loss of connection from our source, haven't we lost a very important part of ourselves? That organic part of us—that part that once lived in harmony with nature, that part of us that could commune with nature around us—the trees, the birds, the land—its gentle slopes and hills—the patchwork of the colors that our 'organic' eyes remain hungry for—and that our soul desires to absorb into itself.

We've made life so complicated with our labor-saving devices. We've built our factories, erected our tall towers, and made ourselves a standard of living that requires a great deal of income to support, and leaves little time left over to enjoy 'life' and living.

Have we made ourselves strangers to our environment? Have we alienated ourselves from the very source of joy and happiness that are to be found in organic life, in exchange for concrete, steel, and electricity?

Some of these things that alienate, such as conveniences—are hard to give up, even if the desire to live a simple life is there. But what can we do, as we seek to 'vacate,' to 're-create'? Maybe find a place that offers us an opportunity to re-acquaint ourselves with the wonder of Nature round about us.

May we seek to re-discover some of the things that brought us a sense of awe and wonder as children; take a journey back to our roots seeking the peace and contentment that can come to us when we slow down and take notice of the beauty of Creation. We might find in our rediscovery of the abundant beauty nature has to offer us that we don't 'need' so much in the way of artificial stimulation as we thought we did.

Wisdom of the Little Drummer Boy

any a time have I wondered how to honor someone in my life that meant a great deal to me? Is the 'gift' something that money can buy? Or must one search and find something singular and unique within oneself? Several years ago, when I found myself wondering, in a stupor, at the Crossroads Mall—trying to come up with the 'ideal gift' I came to my senses. I woke up to the foolishness of my endeavor. A question posed itself in my mind; "why am I doing this?" Why wander around the Mall instead of spending some time with this person I want to honor....

"pa-rum-pa-pum-pum"

In my heart the answer comes: I am my gift to my friend...my time and attention can be my gift to my friend—(and friends). Dinner and candlelight at my house—or concert together — spending 'time' not just money.

"pa-rum-pa-pum-pum"

My gift, my greatest gift is my full attention for a few hours—along with good, nourishing food and music. "We can be our gift to each other," I thought. "Dispense with the store-bought gifts with those who will understand and are 'like-minded'. For others, who can't recognize the value of such a gift—well, a small, meaningful token gift or a gift given to those in need on the friend's behalf. The years have passed.

"pa-rum-pa-pum-pum"

I have honored my friends in this way. Honor has also been bestowed upon me in the same way. The wisdom of the child with his drum prevails.

> "pa-rum-pa-pum-pum"

We have arrived at the season when gift-giving becomes more prominent than any other time of year for many of us. By this time some people have all their Christmas gifts wrapped and ready to be distributed. Others are floundering and uncertain over what to give. I've been reminded of a caring soul, who was floundering and in consternation over what to give; The Little Drummer Boy. He begins his song with hearing news of a king's birth.

> "When they told me,
>
> pa-rum-pa-pum-pum,
>
> A new born king to see,
>
> pa-rum-pa-pum-pum,
>
> I have no gift to bring,
>
> pa-rum-pa-pum-pum,
>
> to lay before the king...."

There were no mega-malls to solve his problem. Nor little gift boutiques or craft-sales. What would one do at such times? It was very important to bring the king a gift—but what?

> "pa-rum-pa-pum-pum"

And then the thought occurred to him to bring a gift that has been bestowed upon him. His Drum! His playing of his drum!

       "pa-rum-pa-pum-pum"

"Shall I play for him?" the child mused.

It was a simple, personal gift. Not costly. But something dear to his heart—that beat, like his heart, with desire to share what he'd been given.

       "pa-rum-pa-pum-pum"

It was a singular, unique offering. A humble offering. You might say—homespun and heart-made.

       "pa-rum-pa-pum-pum"

A gift from his soul.

       "pa-rum-pa-pum-pum."

Stirring Forgotten Memories of a Family Farm

One Saturday afternoon recently, I went to Books Revisited* to attend to a reading by an author from Iowa who grew up on a family farm. The name of his book was "Curlew Home. Essays and a Journey Back".

*Books Revised is a used bookstore in downtown St. Cloud.

Little had I expected that by the time he'd finished reading excerpts from his book, stirring so many of my own memories of growing up on a farm that I'd want to go somewhere and have a good cry.

Tom Montag, the author, wrote simply and down to earth of a wide variety of his experiences and observations: "A man reaches to age where his astonishment up turns his certainty. Old men spend a lot of time sitting on benches and thinking. I was more than fifty years old before I started to understand why. There's a lot for old men to think about. The more you think about it the more astonished you become: how does a fellow get where a fellow is going?"

Do we sit and think enough about where we came from— our roots? As Tom read, memories surfaced in me. The initial memory was my first "return visit" to the farm near Randall, Minnesota where I was born and spent my first four years of life. The house was gone, apparently burned down. Out-buildings remained standing—and "leaning." The farmstead was over-grown with weeds. The old place looked forlorn and forgotten. There was a junk pile by one of the out-buildings that I rummaged through and found a battered and bent oil lamp that I took along with me as a souvenir of my visit. Later, when I talked with my older sister I asked her if she recognized it. "That's Granma's lamp!" she exclaimed. I had in my hand a relic—a tangible relic of my grandmother who'd died in 1937.

As Tom continued to read, more memories surfaced. Tom read on; "Maybe they didn't talk about lonesomeness in those early years—about the day when the young farmer would be planting corn in the near field. His wife would be so lonesome for him, she'd want an excuse to go out and visit with him." I remembered the morning and afternoon breaks in the field, when the women would bring the men coffee and buttered and jammed home-made, sturdy brown bread. They'd sit in the field drinking coffee, eating bread and visiting—straw hats lying beside them—sweat trickling down their tanned dusty faces. It was a good memory. There was a sense of connectedness out there in the field. It was richly peaceful. We belonged to the Earth and that plot of Earth belonged to the family.

Why did I want to cry? It was grief! Grief of loss of those days when the family was connected—when we all sat down to breakfast, dinner and supper together. When I'd go up to the haymow and follow the mews of the newly-born kittens until I'd find where the mother-cat had tried to hide them. I'd spend hours in the haymow with the sweet smell of hay and the warm fuzziness of little kittens. Did I realize how connected I was to the Earth in those days? Of course not, it was all I knew. I knew no other world and took it for granted. Was I happy to live on a farm? I thought not! I wanted to live in town, where there were sidewalks I could roller-skate on and draw hop scotch and bounce a ball and go down to the neighborhood store for a popsicle or Eskimo bar, like my cousins who lived in town. My cousins, however, loved visiting on the farm. When Tom had finished reading, I bought his book and brought it to him to sign. He wrote: "Curlew is everywhere" and so is Randall! So is Little Falls where we moved when my parents lost the mortgage on their farm. Memories of the farm three miles south of

Little Falls and the farm west of Randall live on, newly stirred by another's memories of a farm in Curlew, Iowa.

Many of us who grew up on a family farm didn't realize, at the time, how blessed we were to live so close to the land and to one another. I, for one, grieve the loss of that rich, fertile life…and I will continue, in memory, to visit those forgotten places and be glad that someone came along and stirred up the memories. Thank you, Tom Montag!

Buying Time: An Investment to Consider

We speak, lightly of Time—as Time being of the Essence. And yet, we don't seem to have time for the things and people most important to us. There are pressures upon us we think (mistakenly) that we need to get out of the way first. Once out of the way, we assume, we'll have time for the things important to us. But, unless we're clear about our priorities there will never be time for some things and the people that we need to tend to. These people wait. They're not always aggressive. They try to understand. But oftentimes they cannot understand why a 'job' should be more important than they—the family and friends who love the busy one. As we continue on such a path—giving into pressures that assail us, we gradually, undetectably lose the things that are most important to us through in-attention. We 'lose', not only those we love on the most intimate level, we lose our Dreams. I'm not saying we lose them but we lose the intimacy we once had and could continue to have.

A long time ago a friend in his mid-50's confessed to me, regarding his career, "This was never what I intended to do." He'd lost his Dream—and it now seemed too late to recover. Since it was 'a long time ago' and I was in my mid-20's, I didn't respond as I would have today if someone had said that to me. Today I would have responded, "WELL, what do you plan to do about it now?" I would have challenged him to lay hold of his lost Dream...maybe it wasn't too late.

Loss of money is so often a factor when one dreams of having more time to pursue The Dream. The sad thing is—money wins out too often. There is a mis-conception that we need to remain at our present earning power or increase it. We never think of decreasing it! It's scary to think of giving up a portion of one's income to gain more time. That's when one begins to think, "maybe I'll retire early...Then I'll have the time for those important parts of my life." Consequently one budgets in less time for Family, Friends, and Dreams—willing to sacrifice them on the 'altar of Tomorrow. But for many, that tomorrow never comes. In some cases tomorrow is forgotten, while more income affords more purchasing power for the present, while the purpose of increasing that income for the sake of retiring early sooner gets lost in the muddle of our frantic efforts to buy labor-saving devices, meals out, and little get-away vacations to relieve the pressure of intense work hours, while we take on more hours in order to have more time for Tomorrow. Consequently, it doesn't turn out the way we've planned and we can only hope for that pie-(of time)-in-the-sky-by-and-by.

When my oldest son, Les, died of cancer, I suffered great regret that I hadn't spent more time with him. Although I spent a good deal of time with him, I didn't realize that it hadn't been 'enough' time until he was gone. If only I could have turned back the pages of time and made provisions for someone else to take my place at work. I saw it so clearly…when it was too late. Although I knew Les had understood and accepted my situation, I didn't. What had seemed impossible became possible after the fact—when reality hit. Eight months later I took a certain amount of time off, forced upon me by a serious illness. For two full weeks I was at home, spending most of my time alone—reading, thinking, praying, writing letters, writing in my journal. During that time of retreat a new reality presented itself, "Give up your position as manager and semi-retire." The thought scared me. Cut my income in half…or more? Is that possible? Will it work? But the vision of 'more time' had presented itself. I'd talked much about needing time more than money—although my income was modest. But it became so clear that this was the path. I could not resist or argue with the clarity. That was nine years ago and I haven't experienced a moment of regret. I have this time for the things that are most important to me…time with friends and family…time to keep up my journal, time for letters, calls, and visits with those dear to my heart, time for bread-baking and soup-making and dinners at home with friends. Time for creativity—for the artist part of me to stay alive and well. I'm more fulfilled than I was working full-time, although I loved my job! I knew of no other place I'd rather work than at the Good Earth Co-op, but the shorter hours made it possible to enjoy my work more than when I felt so stretched. In 'buying time' I made a worthwhile investment.

As often as possible I quote a line fro-m an 'ancient' song, "The best things in life are free." And I believe this with all my heart!

Breaking the Pattern...

'**ve** been thinking lately about the way our lives develop into a pattern which we often follow without questioning or stopping to evaluate the purpose for what all we do. We can't easily stand back and look at our lives with objectivity; nor do we always want to. To many of us a pattern is comfortable, something we don't need to give much thought to. For many of us change presents a threat to our old way of doing things. Change requires our attention. In fact, change may even cause for us a need to learn something new; not to mention the added attention we might be required to "pay." But how much are we missing in the process! I've been mulling over in my mind the contents of a book that I listened to on tape: Mutant Messages Form Down Under. It has required much rumination on my part in order that it might be properly "digested." And I had the time to do that because I spent a week home, sick, and was able to give the contents of this book my full attention.

The way I look at physical illness, at least when it happens to me, is that it's an opportunity to be alone and quiet. It's an opportunity to pay attention, to listen to the young and tender shoots of thought that have been, like seeds, in the dark confines of my psyche. Because of past experience, I've come to look upon my illnesses with some degree of expectation, begin to listen more carefully to the "voice within"…just listen.

I've found great benefit in having a book to focus on; something tangible that aids me in drawing from the deeper wells within me. And so Mutant Message…became that tool. This book told of the experience of an American physician, Marlo Morgan, who was accepted into one of the last remaining Aboriginal Tribes in the "out-back" of Australia and who is taken with them for a "walk-about"—a trek through the vast expanses of desert lasting four months. Dr. Morgan did not know this was to be her destiny until it all began to unfold. She had thought perhaps a "little jaunt" and then she would be led back to the jeep that had dropped her off. Well, that didn't happen and she and I had quite a journey! Mine—a vicarious one, her journey was very tangible as she learned the ways of the "last real people" (that's what they call themselves) on earth. They told her that she was one of the "mutants" but honored her in their desire to show her their ways, how they lived, what they believed, etc. Their hope was that she might bring their story to light and share with all other mutants how they'd always lived on the face of this earth of ours, with respect for the land and all its occupants.

No provisions had been made for this four-month journey. They used what they needed along the way: food, water, and shelter. She learned their ancient wisdom, their songs, their respect for the earth and its occupants. The mutual love and camaraderie between the "mutants" and the "real people" was evident throughout the story. I was reminded of a life-changing book I had read years ago—The Savage, My Kinsman—that was so similar to Mutant Messages...

I've often wondered what makes us so called 'civilized' people think that we have something to teach the 'savage' or the Aborigine how to live? I think they might have something to teach us! And this might be a good time to begin to listen, to be more flexible in our thinking, to be more adaptable to new and unfamiliar situations such as Marlo was. She—the student, The Aborigine—the teacher. They, who understood the art of simple living and the one-ness of all beings, they who are the child-like, remind me of a passage in the Bible that speaks of the peaceable Kingdom where "the wolf shall dwell with the lamb, and the leopard shall lie down with the kid...and a child shall lead them" (Isaiah 11:6). We have so much to learn and unlearn about life, about how we fit into the grand plan, about bending and flexibility, about the 'stranger within and the stranger without", and what time spent alone and quiet might open to us. Perhaps it all might serve to break the pattern and show us new things. But it's only when the student is ready that the teacher will appear. Are you ready for your walk-about?

A Mother's Gift

Yes, Phyllis, I guess we can go to *The Wizard of Oz* when it comes to town."

This was a promise my mother made me when I was a child around the age of eight. I don't think that any child of today could have been more excited with the prospect of spending the day at Disneyland or Mall of America than the thrill and anticipation I experienced over the thought of driving in to the big city of Little Falls to attend a matinee (in color, no less!) at the Falls theater. The year was 1939.

My mother, by that time in my life, had made the very deep impression on me that her word was good. This is why I felt no need to remind her, daily, of her promise. It had been my experience that she did not forget what she said she'd do, be it good or bad results for me. I felt confident in waiting for the great occasion in silent anticipation.

I can't remember how many days or weeks of required waiting took place before the Transcript (the local paper) heralded the good news that the Wizard of Oz had begun its showing at the Falls Theatre. Although my mother had not told me the specific day she planned to take me to the movie, I knew that the time was near. I began to count the days in silent hope, knowing that any moment I'd hear my mother say with a tiny twinkle in her eye, "Well, Phyllis, I suppose you better get cleaned up and put your good dress on." I would know why, she would not need to say. Our trips to town were rare.

The last day of the movie arrived, and I continued to wait with unfaltering faith. Nothing had been said about going to the movie since the initial promise was made. There was no need because my mother had never failed in a promise she'd made.

That afternoon I stared with shock and disbelief as I watched my mother move the old wringer wash machine and tubs off the back porch into the kitchen, but then recovered myself when I concluded, "She's just teasing me to make it all the more fun." And I watched her eye for that familiar twinkle and listened for the instructions to get cleaned up. Of course, I was cleaned up, knowing it was the last day of the movie, but was waiting to be told to run and put on my good dress. I watched intently her every move, and when I saw her fire up the old range and begin to put water in the big copper boiler, my heart sank as my mind began to whirl with confusion. "How can this be happening?" I thought. It seemed a point of no return. I knew that my mother would not waste wood or water just to tease. All hope drained out of me and I broke down and sobbed. My mother, turning to me with bewilderment, said, "What's the matter?" I choked out, "You promised to take me to The Wizard of Oz, and today is the last day." Her immediate response was to slap the front of her thigh (her typical gesture of dismay) saying, "I forgot all about The Wizard of Oz!" She didn't say "I'm sorry" or "Another time, maybe," or "Why didn't you remind me?" She simply said, "I forgot…"

The next thing I remember was walking with my mother out of the hot summer afternoon into the cool darkness of the Falls Theatre and the Land of Oz, faith in my mother's word remaining intact.

Little did I realize in my little eight year old mind and heart what a deep impression was being made on me that day. The movie was wonderful but what was greater was my mother's faithfulness to her word. It's the most precious gift my mother gave me…a true legacy.

How tender and fertile the ground of a small child's heart. How powerful a mother's influence.

Facing Our Fears

ou gain strength, courage and confidence by every experience in which you really stop to look fear in the face. You must do the thing which you think you cannot do."*

A friend related to me a recent experience she had with her grandchildren, Shawn (age 4) and Molly (age 2 1/2) regarding a visit they'd made to a near-by park. Molly, who had not been afraid of dogs, children, and swings, suddenly displayed great fear of all three. She kept saying, upon each encounter, "Granma, I'm afraid of kids!" and then "Granma,

*Eleanor Roosevelt

88

I'm afraid of dogs!" and later, when Granma put her on the swing and gave her a push, she wailed, "I'm afraid of going up in the clouds!"

The bewildered Granma returned home with her two charges, and while they sat on the front steps with their popsicles, Granma on one end, Shawn in the middle, Molly began to recite, "I'm not afraid of kids. I'm not afraid of dogs, I'm not afraid to go up in the clouds..." Shawn looked long at Molly, then up into Granma's face, then back to Molly, and said very soberly and quietly, "What else aren't you afraid of, Molly, or aren't you afraid of that, either."

As I listened to my friend's fascinating story, and her grandson's wise question, I couldn't help but think: How very early we begin to deny what we fear. We often dodge the issue, like Molly, and begin to create our own reality as we sit in the safety of our own domain—away from the encounters that trouble us—that make us uncertain of what an invasion of alien creatures such as other children, dogs, and things can do to threaten the homeostasis of our own little world around which we set our personal boundaries.

Most of us know that it's not unusual for a two year old to suddenly become fearful of these things which were once familiar and presented no threat. But because I like the image that the fearful Molly and the wise Shawn revealed about our own human nature...the human condition...I thought if would be a good thing to build on for further philosophizing.

I have been subjected to many fears of late, so I related to this story. Also, my mother used to tell a story about me she thought quite amusing (consequently, I heard it countless times). We were at someone's home—I may have been four or five. I had wondered what was up the stairs beyond the closed door. The reply to my question was "The Boogie-Man" spoken in such a way as to attempt to strike fear in me. But mingled with fear there was curiosity. I replied, "Where's the Boogie-Man? I want to see the Boogie-Man!" Although I don't remember the incident, I am sure of the accuracy of my mother's memory.

As an adult, I've often recalled the story because I've come to realize this is the characteristic element of my reaction to a threatening situation. I find myself quite often in the clutches of one fear or another, where a 'Boogie-Man" could emerge at any moment. But instead of withdrawing, there's a strong impulse to forge ahead and meet the "Boogie-Man" face to face. I do not give in to fear...but that does not mean I'm fearless.

I may experience more fear than the average person because I face what I fear. I do not "hold my head erect and whistle a happy tune so no one will suspect I'm afraid." I don't mind letting others know I'm afraid; in fact, I need to share some of my fears with friends so that I may receive some insight, counsel, and comfort.

To fear is not unhealthy. What is unhealthy is to be guided by one's fears. To hesitate to say or do something needful and important because of fear, to hesitate to have a normal amount of enjoyment because of fear, to hesitate to venture out into uncharted territory because of fear, can do us harm. Fear, if owned and faced can make one richer and stronger. Fear, if yielded to can make one more fearful. Fear can actually make one physically ill, if yielded to too often. Fear can be overcome, as many people with serious phobias have found. It takes a personal choice to resist the power of fear. But let us remember, courage is fear that prays.

So, as Shawn said to Molly, "…and what else aren't you afraid of, or aren't you afraid of that either?"

The Method of the Rose

Some of our easiest platitudes disguise the difficulties of their practice. One of the hardest to follow is the old English maxim that the longest way round is the shortest way there is a particularly difficult one, especially in this age of such passionate faith in the short-cut, in instant happening and instant solutions. There has, perhaps, never been a moment-in-time when the importance of *being* is so neglected in the general preoccupation with *doing*. When there is no realization of the heart, of the unfolding of the human spirit (or that the truth yields to nothing except growth). All of which are the method of the rose.

There is, according to the rose, a time for growth and a time for dormancy. Both require the acquiescence of being. But what if we live in a culture in which 'being' is devalued, while 'doing' is highly valued. Success, achievement, productivity are held in high esteem, and time spent in pursuing such goals gains high honor in most people's assessment as time well spent. But to sit in quiet meditation, reflection and prayer, or to read a good book, these occupations are often disdained with such general responses as "That's nice, but I don't have time for such things."

For one to say "I'm sorry, I can't get together with you this evening, I have to work," is more acceptable than saying, "I'm sorry, I can't get together with you this evening, as I have plans to spend the evening alone in quiet and stillness." And so our time alone, "to be" becomes minute and shifted to the bottom of our personal priorities, when this may be what we need most.

But why must it be so? And why isn't it okay to choose not to answer the phone or the door in order to preserve the place and emptiness in which thoughts that lie too deep for words can be heard and understood in the clarity that comes in silence and quietness? Why must we always obey the nagging voice of the collective consciousness that speaks so authoritatively and matter-of-factly, reminding us that wise use of our time is to *accomplish*, to *achieve*, to *attain*, to *produce*. We must have something to show for our lives; whether it is a degree, a badge, or some merit of honor to put on display and show the world that we have this value, this worth.

It is not my desire or intention to devalue the pursuit of great things, of fulfilling worthy goals, of finding some purpose in life that will bring some benefit to ourselves and others. My desire and aim is to strike a balance in regard to the great value that lies in those devalued empty spaces of each life where we can connect with our inner, passive being and listen carefully to its wisdom. "We need rest, times of respite, to help us understand ourselves, and the meaning of our relationship with others. We can understand this better if we explore the relationship of rests in music and their relationship to the melody. It is part of the order and expressive meaning of music. If the rests were taken out, all would be cacophony."*

Out of stillness, reflection, listening and yielding to the silence comes an unfolding, a greater awareness and deeper and richer experience of life, bringing greater meaning to the work and the activities in which we engage. Therefore, we may grow (in the shortest way) by taking time for dormancy like all the growing things round about us.

Thankfulness

he approach of November and the celebration of Thanksgiving day brings with it many various points of view about how to celebrate it, with whom to celebrate it, and whether or not to celebrate it at all. But most of us, I find, make some sort of plans around Thanksgiving Day, as it's a day off many people, while it's a long weekend for others.

*Diane D. Gautney

93

The question then arises: How might I creatively use this particular day as I gather with friends and/or family (or sit alone) in a more productive way than "just" stuffing myself full of good food and then giving in to a few hours in front of the TV or a snooze?

Thanksgiving Day, I understand, is to give thanks for the Harvest...the abundance that the earth has yielded the past year..."for the fullness thereof." One thing for which we can be most thankful—that it was a beautiful summer, rain, sun and reasonably mild weather. Very few complaints I heard about the past "Minnesota summer," and much in the way of thankfulness for how good it's been.

But sometimes it's the little things, like one lone maple leaf that shimmered with color and beauty lying in my path when I walked. I picked it up and put it in my pocket to take it with me. Later, I ran into a friend I hadn't seen for a while. My friend was exhibiting frustration over a problem that had just developed. I took the maple leaf out of my pocket and handed it to him. It seemed to melt him—to bring about a small turning point.

Why do we often focus on the negative side—fuming and fussing over things as they are, when a little light-hearted-ness might be of more help to each other. A word of cheer, a hand on the shoulder, or a little hug or pat given or received might become a source of 'Thanksgiving' for us.

This is not meant to negate the stark realities of life—the suffering that many are enduring daily, i.e., the floods, earth-quakes, tornadoes and hurricanes not to mention the wars going on in many parts of the world, and the general state of our planet, etc. But we need strength to bear the weight of these problems, and a thankful heart might be the antidote we need for the news that seeps into our lives via TV, radio, newspapers, and weekly magazines, as well as our own daily trials.

Take in the beauty around you! The beauty of the sky and its constantly changing face. The beauty of the vivid autumn colors as they slowly give way to starkness and whiteness of winter. The beauty of a single snowflake. The beauty of the face of a child. The beauty of the face of a beloved friend.

As we receive all the beauty that the world has to offer, it will not be too difficult to "celebrate" Thanksgiving, whether we do it with a large stuffed turkey, gathering with friends and relations, or whether we sit quietly alone with meager fare, our Thanksgiving will feed us well.

In Search of Inner Wisdom

e seem now to be moving out of an era where we sought answers to mental, emotional, and physical problems outside of our selves. We've sought knowledgeable 'experts' who would tell us what to do and how to do it. Mostly we've been pumped full of various pills and medicines that have often created side effects that are worse than the disease due to their cumulative effect. We have come to believe in the 'quick-fix' approach to our various maladies, and we have paid dearly for this folly. Many of us have, as a result, become disillusioned with the experts and have begun taking responsibility for our own lives.

The resulting burden of responsibility for our own lives has driven us within for answers. Many of us have found resources we hadn't before comprehended—a unique consciousness about our lives and life in general continues to unfold. Lo and behold! We find ancient truths that have survived, i.e. the remedies and therapies we seem to be finding effective have been in use since the dawn of history.

The methods of healing that were employed were of minimal nature—simple activities such as talking, touching, listening, being silent in order to help the sick person. These tools involved a certain way of being. So much of our need, whether mental, physical, emotional or spiritual, lies in just being. We need time, we need rest, we need space in order to work through our problems. We also need support of friends and family.

But there are many people, sad to say, who continue to buy into the quick-fix approach, simply due to the pressure of time. However, these people who are having a race with time are realizing that a quick-fix is only an illusion, and the fix isn't long lasting. Therefore we must simply take time to seek the meaning in the various illnesses that move into our bodies, and our minds, and our neighborhoods, and our communities. These illnesses are messengers, and we haven't always taken the time to stop and read the messages they bear. We treat the symptoms but don't seek the cause…like disconnecting the smoke alarm when it sends out its messages while the fire rages on.

Larry Dosey, MD, writes, "…Let us take a look at modern medicine. Modern medicine is a here-and-now term. It implies a medicine that is recent, up-to-date, contemporary, and 'now' as opposed to ancient, antiquated and old fashioned forms of therapy whose time has passed. Our concept of 'modern' requires a linear time, a time in which the 'now' is safely walled off from the past and future, the flowing time of common sense."

Common sense is such a comfortable, old fashioned, basic term. Common sense, according to Aristotle, is 'to know what's true.' Knowing what's true comes as a result of being, waiting, listening for messages from within us to come to the surface. It requires allowing time and space for the unconscious within us to become conscious. It is as it were giving birth to the truth from within us.

We need to abandon seeking information and help from the 'experts' as we turn inward for that inner wisdom that each individual among us possesses. Balance comes into play here. We need the balance that comes as a result of being open to all sources of truth and then sorting through.

So let us mine the gold and other treasure that lay hidden in the deep crevices and caves of our unconscious being. Let us tune into some of that ancient wisdom that fosters common sense. We may not always find a cure, but we're more likely to find a healing.

Take Time

If time could be made into a commodity that could be bought and sold, it might be more precious than gold. We struggle with our twenty-four hour day trying to lengthen it by turning back the clock, developing time-savers, budgeting time to try and make it stretch to cover all the needs of our day. Generally, our reason or excuse, for not doing what we wanted to do, is because of lack of time rather than lack of money, strength, or desire. Time, therefore, or lack of it, seems to be our greatest limitation. "If only we had more time…" we often lament.

However when we do happen to find ourselves with some unexpected time on our hands, we often misuse or waste it. Times such as a broken appointment or an expected guest being unable to come at the last minute, or those many times when we find ourselves having to wait for someone—these little spaces of time might come to us as unexpected gifts. If only we could be a little more prepared to recognize these moments as an opportunity to lean back and relax, maybe read a book that we've carried with us, take a mini-retreat from the hustle and bustle of life, clear our thoughts and let some of the tensions drain off…contemplate. If we look upon these little spaces of time as something of value, that way we might look on it as a bank-error in our favor or an unexpected dividend or a refund that comes in the mail, we might be more apt to take advantage of these moments instead of letting them slip away unused.

Priority is another aspect. What do I truly value? And am I using my energies and free-time toward what is important to me? Do I recognize the opportunities that come clothed in other forms? I hope so. I really desire to make better use of the time I have. And you?

...to light one candle...

ublic consciousness is being raised in regard to chemicals, pesticides, and poisons that are saturating our food, our bodies, our earth and our atmosphere. Leading magazines such as Time, Newsweek, and National Geographic, and broadcasts such as 60 Minutes, and 20/20 are telling us that we are slowly being poisoned, clogged up and suffocated by invisible enemies to our health.

As we gradually awaken to the TRUTH, we have varying individual responses to that truth. Some of us lament, "What's the use? It's too late!" Some of us respond with the quizzical attitude of a doubting Thomas. "I don't know...I need more proof." Some of us feel as if awakening from a coma—a Rip-Van-Winkle-40-year sleep, "W-h-a-t-s-h-a-p-p-e-n-i-n-g?" Still some of us would like to turn over and go back to sleep as we say to the other person in the room, "Pull down the shades and close the door behind you!"

However some of us have hope that the tide of poisons, chemicals, and pesticides can be turned—that each of us can find our own little 'niche' to help and influence the world around us and begin to do our part. We need to remember, "It's better to light one little candle than to curse the darkness."

As we seek that 'niche' of influence and help, we might consider these suggestions: become an ENVIRONMENTAL SHOPPER—avoid using disposable goods such as flash-light batteries, throw-away containers, throw-away lighters, non-returnable or recyclable bottles, etc., and buy as many reusable products as possible. Avoid wasteful packaging. Recycle WHENEVER possible. Plastics, glass, aluminum, newspaper, tin, cardboard, steel are all recyclable. Start a compost heap in your yard for all organic material. Help influence our local growers and farmers to grow their products organically (pesticide and chemical free) by selecting and preferring organic produce, legumes, and grains. Walk, bike, car-pool, and use public transportation whenever possible.

Last but not least, learn more about what's happening to our earth, water, and sky by paying closer attention to information offered through public radio, television, magazines, leaflets, etc. Share what you're learning with friends, relatives, co-workers, teachers, students, etc. Tap the brains of people in the know by asking questions. Attend meetings of the St. Cloud Environmental Council. Read books written by authors who have been forerunners in understanding the elements of ecology and sustainable agriculture such as Aldo Leopold, who developed the notion of a "land ethic" and argued that "humans cannot escape responsibility for its well-being." He wrote one small book, <u>Sand Country Almanac</u>. Wendle Berry, Wes Jackson, and Bruce Coleman co-authored <u>Meeting the Expectation of the Land</u>, and Russell Lord "evokes a deep feeling for the unity of life as it's properly related to the ever-renewing earth" in his book <u>The Care of the Earth.</u>

All of these books, and more, are available at our local library, as well as our local bookstores. We can't do all and be all but we can share our own light and do our own small part.

Uncovering Treasured Memories

When my youngest son was in the process of leaving home and furnishing his apartment, I gave him a ladder-back chair he liked. It was, however, in need of refinishing, and he went at the job with much zeal. Once in a while I'd glance toward the patio where he was working. It was a hot summer day. I realized that removing the red enamel paint was not an easy job. I also thought about when I painted it thirty-five years before, and how much easier it was to put on the paint than it was to take it off.

I apologized to my son for having put the paint on in the first place, making his job so hard. "But," I said, "We were covering up everything back in those days." As I made this statement an underlying truth burst forth; "Yes, we were covering up everything!" And in this burst of new awareness of the deeper meaning of that statement, I thought of how this present generation is working hard to uncover all the past generation covered with paint and with other means...

I recently visited Landmark Center in St. Paul, a charming and historical building. Reading in the brochure about the cover-up and restoration, it was almost impossible to believe that beautiful old ceilings had been hidden by dropped ceilings and fluorescent lights, and how the marble on the main floor had been painted green and how a stained glass skylight had been painted to cover it. One can't help but wonder whatever possessed people to paint over beautiful wood, marble, and stained glass. What madness!

But, it isn't hard to understand when one thinks of the Great Cover-up of so many things. Partly, it seems, because we were so 'future oriented,' had such great hope in the future, while the past was so full of mistakes, pain and failures. We were glad to cover it up. By so doing we would put it behind us and forget—and escape.

Things don't work that way. It was the proverbial "throwing out the baby with the bath water." Yes, the past may have been full of mistakes, pain, and failures. But our past is full of golden moments and memories. Our past is the rich and fertile soil out of which we grow into the present and the future. The past is full of hidden treasures covered over with red and green paint and other garish coverings. Treasures lie buried under the rubble of plastic and polyester and other imitation materials that offer no warmth or comfort.

We long to rediscover and reconnect ourselves with the past. That longing is revealed in many ways, the least of which is shown through the current nostalgia quest for antiques and other memorabilia. The greatest of which are the haunting memories of.

Share your memories as you gather together. Laugh over them, weep over them, and ponder them. Above all, bring them with you into the future. Therein lie many rich and wonderful forgotten parts of ourselves.

Tending Our Machines or Gardens?

Those of us who gave our undivided attention to Bill Moyer's series, "Healing and The Mind" on channel 2 this past month, found it well worth our while. The emphasis was placed on the mental and spiritual aspects of our being rather than the nutritional aspect. Maybe this is because we are in need of a 'balance'. The phrase "you are what you eat" misleads us. We are more, much more than that.

Bill Moyers talked of how Chinese Medicine addresses the needs of the body compared to western medicine. The Chinese look upon the body as a garden. Western medicine looks upon the body as a machine. We tend to and nurture a garden. We fix a machine. Machines and gardens both produce, but in different ways. Do we really want to see ourselves as machines?

A machine is a machine is a machine...

A garden has potential to become a work of art, a place of beauty, a source of nourishment, an opportunity for a relationship between the gardener and the garden. It brings forth riches from the soil, the air, the rain, and cooperates with a seed to create a great value.

I do not mean to disparage machines, but I do not wish to identify myself with one either. I wish to think of myself as a garden.

Wendell Barry wrote a collection of essays entitled <u>What are People For</u>? In this collection he calls us back to our basic identity. He helps us to find, again, what is important so we might examine our own lives and sort out the essential from the non-essential in our existence. We need such writings to help us call to our remembrance what life is all about—what we, as human beings, are about.

We have been so steeped in the technological age that we actually begin to think in mechanical terms, fine tuning ourselves until we look upon ourselves as machines.

Let us, with the Chinese, look at ourselves from this perspective, a garden, having a Gardener, a well tended garden in the process of becoming.

There is a need for wholeness, for balance. Healing will be the result of wholeness. We may be healed, through not cured. And we may be cured but not healed.

'Ex-stressing' Yourself

One Christmas, several years ago, I moved a flourishing English Ivy to the landing on the stairs in order to have a place to put our Christmas tree. When Christmas was over I was dismayed to find that my once healthy and radiant beautiful plant was quite sick and under attack by spider mites who had woven their little webs all over the leaves. Though I did what I could to rescue it from the attack, my ivy gradually died. And I was mystified. "What had caused this strong healthy plant to succumb," I pondered, "after all the years I'd fed and nourished it?" I didn't have a clue. Several years later the answer came to me.

Only after I've given much thought to the subject of the Immune System, did the memory of my lovely plant come back to me. What I have concluded about the ivy is that the change in environment, the lack of loving attention, created the stress that broke down its immune system. I'd come to realize that change whether it creates a happy or sad emotional response, puts our bodies under stress. And stress, according to most experts in the field tends to break down the immune system. Stress comes to us in many forms and down many avenues. Most of us are so used to living under stress that we're conditioned to believe it is a normal part of life—a necessary evil. One of the definitions of stress is: "bodily or mental tension resulting from factors that alter an extant equilibrium". Simply put—to be thrown off balance. Stress is, also, the perception of threat, a person sensing that he is inadequate to cope, helplessness; "Not only have I messed up my life, I've messed up the world!"

And what is the greatest buffer against stress? Social support. People who are lonely have less ability to trigger an immune response that would protect their bodies. Stress occurs on three levels: personal, interpersonal, and transpersonal. According to Dr. Dean Ornish (who wanted to call his book Open Heart instead of Reversing Heart Disease, but whose publisher wouldn't allow it) we need to have an open heart toward others.

Much of our stress has to do with our approach to life, and how we see ourselves, each in our individual role. Whether we embrace life or shrink from it will affect our immune system. Whether we blame others and circumstances rather than taking responsibility for our own 'story' and the part we play will make the difference between our health and illness, both mental and physical.

To be mindful, to live *in* the moment rather than *for* the moment, to be in tune and in harmony with our environment and with others who occupy a certain amount of space within that environment will draw strength into ourselves and energize our immune system, as well. We will, as a result, exude health and heartiness.

My English Ivy offered me a lesson through its life and death. I hope to grow more mindful of the messages that come to me in many ways and from varied sources. We have many teachers. And when we are ready to learn, the teacher will come.

Reassessing Our Relationships

As summer approaches and we move outdoors, there is the reenactment of greater involvement with our neighbors through backyard and sidewalk conversations. Some of these meetings are a welcome encounter, some are not—especially if our neighbors are the four-legged, six-legged-multi-legged and often times winged variety.

Many of us have armed ourselves against such unwelcome neighbors who intrude upon our premises uninvited. Our combative methods of ridding ourselves of these pesky neighbors have been abundant. We swat, we spray, we poison, and we trap. We also saturate our bodies with various chemicals in order to make ourselves less desirable to these obnoxious, and often times insistent creatures.

However, there may be a better way of encountering these critters...a way that certain people down through history have dealt with these invaders. Most of us are familiar with Albert Schweitzer and St. Francis of Assisi, who learned the secret of peaceful co-existence with those that seem to insist on staking a claim in our...OUR territory!

The Ancient Mariner who unthinkingly killed an albatross, suffered the consequences of his dark deed. The guilt of the act weighed upon him feeling as if the dead albatross hung from his neck. Awareness of his act had dawned upon him and he realized, "I had done a hellish thing..." Although this consciousness came too late for the albatross, the Mariner was to realize that he could actually love the "slimy things" that lived in the sea when he saw them in a new light, with heightened consciousness.

> "O happy living things" No tongue
>
> their beauty might declare:
>
> A spring of love gushed from my heart,
>
> And I blessed them unaware.
>
> "The self same moment I could pray;
>
> And from my neck so free
>
> The Albatross fell off, and sank
>
> Like lead into the sea."

This awareness of The Ancient Mariner caused him to utter the words we all know so well: "He loveth best who loveth all. Both creatures great and small."

Maybe we need some great paradigm shift in regard to "these creatures, great and small." Maybe we could, like the Mariner, learn to like them, as we take time to gaze upon their intricate beauty, and identify with their struggle for existence in our common world.

J. Allen Boone, journalist and author of Kinship with All Life and Adventures in Kinship with All Life, was a modern-day St. Francis. He learned the value of a humility that opens to us the privilege of seeing that there is "in reality, no separating barriers between one living thing and another." He began to find the lost link, "the linkage which ever holds all life together in inseparable kinship and oneness."

Let us seek to communicate with these neighbors of ours. Maybe we can learn something from them, and they from us…maybe.

Needs of the Heart

hen it comes to health and wholeness, there is more than meets the eye…at least the physical eye. There is also the 'inner' eye that sees our inner needs. These needs, if met or not met, contribute to the condition of the whole person.

Therefore, rather than speaking of the value of good nutrition through healthy eating, and the merits of herbal remedies and nutritional supplements, let's take time to direct our attention to our 'inner needs.'

One of our greatest needs that began before birth is the need for relatedness, the comfort that comes through friendship, intimacy, kinship, call it what you will. But to narrow it down, let's focus on the subject of the deeper need that goes beyond hugs, soft fuzzies, and warm pats.

Who and what we are, at the very core of our being, is dependent on our own sense of self-worth, that we either develop or don't develop. To learn to be 'friends' with one's self is a personal responsibility. No one else in the world can meet that need. But some degree of our self-worth or lack thereof, has to do with those in our lives with whom we are on most intimate terms, often that significant other. If there is any degree of openness with another we become more vulnerable to the effect that approval or disapproval will have.

Relationships are no longer built on the kind of common bonds that people had forty and more years ago when the common bond was working the land and raising a family. Not everything was ideal, but working toward a common goal tended to cement the bonds of loyalty and comradery. But nowadays we've attempted to become independent, so independent that we no longer need one another, or that's what we'd like to think. We, in fact, work very hard on independence rather than striking the balance that engenders a deep relationship.

In our striving for individuality, we tell ourselves we don't 'need' anyone. As a result, relationships flounder and fail, lacking that common bond that keeps us together. And so we isolate and insulate ourselves against intimacy that may hurt us, and then starve deep down inside for tender words that convey the love of a loyal companion. But if the love is really there, words aren't always needed. Remembering the words from Old Love, a song sung by folk artists Neal and Leandra: "We don't need to say 'I love you' but we say it anyway."

As the month of February and Valentine's Day comes around again, reminding us of 'heart-felt' love, it might be good to reflect on these inner needs we all have, and some of us own up to, to meet and be met on a deeper level, even if it might make us more vulnerable to pain. That's not so bad if the price of pain offers something better than isolation. Health and wholeness is more than food.

Meaning and Being; a Vital Link to Wholeness

Approximately ten years ago I experienced some major changes in my life within the framework of a six month time period. I gave no consideration at the time to my immune system and knew nothing of the ways in which mental and emotional stress can break it down.

During that period of time a friend suggested I take a written test that was designed to reveal where one stands in regard to the danger of major health problems following a period of the stress of change in one's life. My score was very high revealing that I was at great risk for major health problems. My friend who'd worked with these tests and was familiar with their reliability counseled me to rest, reflect and recuperate from these shifts in my life.

Prior to her counsel I'd not given 'resting' any consideration, since some of these changes had actually removed pressures from my life. My only thought had been to 'switch gears' and fill up the void with some new activity. But being aware of my friend's wisdom and experience, I took her advice. Although I experienced some degree of illness as the test predicted, I fared quite well. I also enjoyed this retreat from life and look back on it with found memories.

Since that time I've become increasingly interested in the Mind-body connection in regard to health and wholeness. Around the same time Bernie Siegel, MD, was the most visible and popular proponent of the Mind-Body connection authoring the well known book <u>Love, Medicine, and Miracles</u>. There were, however, other medical doctors pioneering in the same field who were not so well known, such as Larry Dossey, MD, who wrote <u>Space, Time, and Medicine</u>, and Blair Justice, psychologist, who authored <u>Who Gets Sick? Thinking and Health</u>. Others were continuing to emerge and come forth with important data on the Mind-Body Connection.

Recent books on the subject are numerous beyond mention. However, I will mention Joan Borysenko, MD, who opens up new vistas to wholeness in her book <u>Fire in the Soul</u> in which she weaves threads of her own history with others who are finding the path of wholeness through resolution of mental, emotional, and spiritual issues. Larry Dossey, MD, has several books on the subject of Mind-Body. Two of these are <u>Meaning and Medicine</u> and <u>Healing Words</u>. The latter documents that prayer is as valid and vital a healing tool as surgery.

Our concern for good nutrition must not and need not be abandoned in light of this new awareness regarding Mind-Body. Dean Ornish, MD, writes with a wide scope of vision as he addresses health and wholeness in his book on the subject, <u>Reversing Heart Disease</u>, encompassing all of the factors that aid us in achieving good health.

Those of you who are seeking various ways and means toward wholeness might gain great benefit in making any of the above mentioned books part of your reading, reflection, and retreat.

In Search of Joy

I've been getting acquainted recently with the Greek god, Dionysus. The opening paragraph of the book that introduced me to Dionysus reads thus: "Ecstasy, the Dionysian experience, may be intellectually unfamiliar. But in ecstatic expression we will recognize a long forgotten part of ourselves that makes us truly alive and connects us with every living thing. In Greek myth, that part of ourselves is Dionysus."*

I'm reminded, too, of a part of The Lion King. It was said of Simba, the main character; "He's forgotten who he is."

Mr. Darling, the father of the three children in the story of Peter Pan, had forgotten his experience as a child of being carried away into Never-Never Land by Peter Pan, until it happened to his children.

Sometimes, I have these flashes these moments of truth, when I realize that I've forgotten who I am! Especially when I sit on a park bench, as I am doing at the present, watching my granddaughter, Stephanie, frolic in the grass and hop on the rocks. I realize that the adult in me has been holding the child in me a prisoner.

I've thought much about what it is that characterizes a child. A child is a free spirit that cares little for what others think of their actions. A child, also, is quite unconcerned about others' actions, unless they are completely outrageous! A child is spontaneously joyful. A child is

*Robert Johnson, Ecstasy

sensuous…experiencing the world through the senses. A child loves discovery. A child can both laugh and cry with energy and gusto.

Adults esteem thinking and doing as progress and success. All this has been won at the expense of feeling, intuition, caring, receptivity. Adults are uptight about how things are going, and if they are going in the right direction. Adults are rational and serious. They know what's what and who's who. At least they think they do, or act as if they think they do. They try to figure out everything!

A child is spirited, abandoned, and celebrates life. A child is an ideal Dionysian spirit. The Dionysian spirit is the life force! It is indomitable joyful energy.

"The vibrant energy of the earth inevitably triumphs over human efforts to suppress it, just as the trees' growing roots will eventually burst thought a concrete sidewalk that has been laid over them.

My desire for all of us who have forgotten who we are is that we will be inspired by the child-like quality of the Dionysian spirit and let go of our adult agendas, as much as possible, and let our imprisoned child get out and frolic in the grass, and skip on the rocks, breaking out of old, rigid, predictable patterns as we search for joy.

...A Very Good Place to Start

In our aim and desire for relationship to others, in our aim to be understood and to understand, we use two main vehicles of expression—conversation and communication.

As we wish to avoid relationship with others, we may use talk as a means of avoidance. Talking does not necessarily establish either communication or conversation. It can, in fact, be a smoke screen to keep people at a distance.

Conversation: Oral exchange of sentiments, observations, ideas or opinions.

Communication: An act or instance of transmitting information communicated...a process by which information is exchanged between individuals through a common system of symbols, signs or behavior.

Talk: To deliver or express in speech...to influence, affect or cause by talking...speak.

The last line in the definition of communication is an important one. It denotes that we may, inadvertently, be communicating when we are neither talking nor conversing. It is believed that over 60% of our conversation is through behavior (body language).

With these things in mind, let us proceed to give some attention to the way each one of us, as an individual, communicates. What do I want others to know about me and my feelings and thoughts? What do I want to know about others and their feelings and thoughts? How interested am I in genuine communication? Is it a goal in my life, in my relationships with friends and family, or do I wish to remain on an impersonal level in most of my relationships for fear of vulnerability?

Realizing that there is much diversity in our aims in our relationships, I will try to take aim at one particular issue. This issue keeps coming up in conversations, as a vital key in all communication: the fact that we are communicating, whether we are aware or not, through our behavior toward others. By our respect and courtesy, or lack thereof, on all levels. This is a "silent" language, a language that speaks louder than words. It's a language that can either elevate another's self-esteem or else knock the pins out from underneath them. Nothing was said, but communication took place nevertheless. It can be a look, a turn of the head, a gesture of the hand, a movement of the body that speaks volumes. There may be eye contact or lack of it. But whatever we do we need to be clear that we are either mindful or mindless in the effect we have on others.

Our presence, the tone of voice, the manner that we express toward others can convey more than we were ever aware. The point is that we need to take time to consider what we want to communicate. By being aware, by being "mindful" in every situation in which we find ourselves, we will be able to develop our communication skills to a level that reveals how we regard others. Courtesy and respect are worthy goals to pursue in all of our relationships whether close or distant. With these goals in mind, we may find ourselves in tune with ourselves and with others. And we may be laying a foundation to build on in developing any potential relationship.

'Relationship' may extend to all life, beginning with one's relationship to one's self and extending outward to encompass all the animate and inanimate. Our behavior and attitudes toward ourselves will be revealed in the way we relate to our friends and family, our environment and our planet. "Let's start at the very beginning, a very good place to start."

Reviving the Tradition of Christmas

What is the first thought that comes to your mind at the mention of Christmas? Tree-lights-gifts-pine boughs-cookies-carols-gathering with family and friends around a cozy fire-place and concerts-sending and receiving cards and greetings? Or is your first thought time shortage, money shortage, stress, pressure, obligations, weariness, loneliness, meaninglessness? None of the above? All of the above?

As another season-to-be-jolly rolls around, I'm inclined again to talk about the meaning of it all...an on, on, on, going search for a sane, sensible, yet significant way of celebrating the season—a way of carving one's own path without disappointing or offending friends and family who depend on us to continue with past traditions.

Although I've shared a bit of my own story in past Christmas Newsletters, I call to mind these past several years since I've dispensed with the commercialism of the season—choosing rather to get together with friends and family as we give ourselves to each other in our own very unique way. It has been very good—much better than the stress I'd experienced when I conformed to the tradition of gift exchange, and how, as we gather for cozy times at home or attend some of the lovely Christmas concerts that are offered during the season. For me it's truly been a time of peace and enjoyment.

A message to those who plunge into the season with the idea that there are no options to the way you've been celebrating the Christmas season. There are options. And maybe a great majority of people, i.e. your family and friends, would be more than happy to look at other options. This is a good time to talk about it. Also to reminisce over past Christmases together and decide what you found of value to keep, and what to change to improve the 'celebration'.

One last thought in regard to the gift-giving tradition, especially for those of us who already have more than we need. Aim that desire and initiative to give gifts toward a family or families whom you know to be in need. Share your abundance with them, remembering that "it's more blessed to give than to receive." No doubt most of us know of such people. If we don't, there are those abroad…

This little treatise is not designed to change anyone's mind in regard to Christmas Tradition, as much as it is to aid in examining our own values and thoughts on the subject and to avoid the herd instinct, and become more thoughtful about what we do and why we do what we do. So, what is the first thing that comes to your mind at the mention of Christmas?

Reliving Old Stories

elen Luke said, "A real story touches not only the mind, but also the imagination and the unconscious depths in a person." Harold Goddard stated in his book The Meaning of Shakespeare, "The Destiny of the world is determined less by the battles that are lost and won, but by the stories it loves and believes in."

We are approaching the celebration of old stories in these coming weeks and days! Thanksgiving, Hanukkah, Christmas. The continuation of these celebrations must mean that the majority of us love and believe in them, in spite of the overlay of commercialism. Many of us retain our childhood memories of these festive times, and hope to retain some of the essence of joy we experienced as children when these days and the sheer expectancy of these days drew near. There were friends and relatives from far and near filling the house. Also filling the house was the aroma of baked goods mingled with other sizzling delicacies roasting in the oven. There was, in general, excitement mingled with the pent up emotions of waiting for the day to come.

The celebration of Thanksgiving, which dates back to 1674, was over the joy of the harvest and the gathering in of the bounty of the earth, the beauty of the colors of the apples and pumpkins and squash and corn, all of the other produce that stores through the winter months. A good harvest was a thing for which to be truly thankful, especially when we didn't have grocery stores and supermarkets carrying produce shipped from around the world.

And so, as a result of modern day technology and our pace of life, we've lost the meaning of the celebration, but continue with the motions.

Could we, somehow, impregnate new meaning for our time into this old celebration? Instead of just going through the motions we might reflect on what we have to be thankful for. We could possibly ask each guest around the table to bring some token of Thanksgiving…something that has been reflected on the week prior to the celebration—a poem, an object, a song, a personal writing. Such sharing can touch other hearts and mutual Thanksgiving may be the result.

Then there are the celebrations of Christmas and Hanukkah with their many and various symbols: the STAR that lights the way of the wise, the GIFTS bestowed, and the commitment to REMEMBER a certain time in history that had great importance to a people.

There are other symbols that have evolved from the original Christmas Story—the Christmas tree and decorations, the holly, the candles, the exchange of gifts and many other collective and individual symbols that have accumulated over the years.

If we can only, consciously, celebrate the meaning of these coming holidays, the meaning and the symbols, thereof, we may find our experience enriched…lest "we have the experience but miss the meaning."

Savoring the Simple Things

I've always been somewhat mystified by the way some people eat a candy bar: two bites, and it's gone. The reason I'm mystified is because I've been conditioned to believe that candy and other tasty morsels, are meant to be savored.

How one approaches small things like candy and tasty morsels may indicate, on a small scale, how we approach life on the larger scale, i.e., how we live our lives and the philosophy behind our attitude and actions. Take, for instance, the White Rabbit in Alice in Wonderland. All we seem to know about him is that he is always looking at his watch and always rushing "somewhere." He is definitely not oriented toward taking life at a slower pace, stopping to smell the roses, and savoring life. He is definitely under great stress, fearing that his "head will roll" if he isn't at a certain place at a certain time. And, figuratively, he's already "lost his head" with worry.

As we approach this New Year with its new opportunities, we might do well to reorient our thinking and our approach to life and adopt a beginner's mind, the child-like mind, full of awe and wonder as each new day brings hidden gifts if we can but notice their presence in our lives. Enter with me into the world of Christopher Robin and Pooh Bear (funny old bear) and drink in the joy that living in the moment can bring. "Life itself, when understood and utilized for what it is, is sweet," according to Pooh. He understood that, and he brought honey along on his journeys. His philosophy is always, "Lucky I brought this with me. Many a bear going out on a warm day like this could never have thought of bringing a little something with him." What we bring with us in life determines the difference. It's also good, as we approach life, to approach it with a desirable companion, someone who appreciates what we appreciate, as was the case of Rat and Mole in <u>The Wind and the Willows</u>. Here's how their paths crossed:

"As he sat on the grass and looked across the river, a dark hole in the bank opposite just above the water's edge, caught his eye, and dreamily he fell to considering what a nice snug dwelling place it would make for an animal with few wants and fond of a bijou riverside residence, above flood level, remote from the dust. As he gazed, something bright and small seemed to twinkle down in the heart of it, vanished and twinkled once more like a tiny star. But it could hardly be a star in such an unlikely situation. Than as he looked, it winked at him, and so it declared itself to be an eye, and a small face began to grow up around it, like a frame around a picture. It was a water rat."

Ultimately Rat took Mole on a journey that brought both adventure and joy. He was an apt companion for Mole. Had Mole not stopped to sit on the river bank, he'd not have encountered the one who became his good and dear friend. And so it is with our own lives. There is great need to slow to a stop and experience our surroundings, letting time pass, waiting for whatever might emerge. We need that kind of approach to life in our daily experience lest we fail to notice the little and great treasurers waiting to be noticed, waiting to be savored. The wisdom of Rat in the wild wood unfolds when he says, "We must make a start, and take our chances, I suppose. The worst of it is, I don't exactly know where we are. And now this snow makes everything so different." Before us lies an uncharted path, a New Year, and maybe the best place to find ourselves is "not knowing where we are" as we adopt the "beginner's mind"...ultimate simplicity.

Getting from Here to There

ecently I've been reminded of my involvement in a discussion that a group of women were having on the subject of computerized dating. I believed that the conversation struck in my mind because I became aware of a truth that had evaded me up until then: i.e. how each of us gets from 'here' to 'there.'

The women were having a discussion about computer-generated matchmaking. I found myself quite fascinated by the subject, and by a story that was being told of how well it had worked for one couple. Then another woman began praising the value of computerized matchmaking. Since I have never been computer-friendly, I wasn't qualified to join in the discussion. But I listened, with a somewhat skeptical but open mind to what others had to say. (I've found that one learns much more by listening than talking although I'm always ready to throw in my two-cents worth whenever I have an opportunity to do so.). As I listened, I realized the absolute impossibility of my being able to adapt to that particular philosophy, because I had my own philosophy about life that didn't fit with the ideas I was hearing. This is not to say that others were wrong in their way of thinking regarding the vast magical powers that this computer-age offers us in finding directions and solutions to whatever one might be in quest of.

It was at that point that I began realizing how very much I liked my own philosophy regarding romantic encounters; Why not just let our lives 'unfold' as each of us moves toward our own unique destiny? To give credibility to my philosophy, or 'belief system,' it has been my modus operandi for many years, and it has worked well for me. I don't 'believe' in trying to steer myself toward a worthy goal of some kind. I believe in saying "yes" to whatever life has handed me…not that I haven't had many struggles and often times downright resistant to what life was handing me, as I moved, often painfully, down Destiny's road. The simple fact is that it is my core belief that I'll reach my Destination by learning to accept-what-is, to look at what 'appear' as obstacles, threatening forces and bewildering twists and turns, as transformational aids, as I continue on this path that leads me toward my own bliss. "Follow your bliss," said Joseph Campbell. My translation of that is: "Follow your dream." Follow YOUR dream, not someone else's!

I've been troubled, often, by all of the how-to-books that are being peddled on the market-of-life. "How to get from Here to There in ten or seven easy steps." These experts say, "It worked for me and it can work for you too, besides I can make a little money on the side, on my way to fame." Don't mis-understand what I say regarding 'How-to' books. They're not all in the same category—and there are many that have some merit. But no one but me can be acquainted with my personal desires, Bliss, or Dream as it continues to unfold. No one else can hand me their dream and say, "Here, try this out for size…it worked for me!"

The greatest obstacle to following one's own dream that leads each one of us to our own true destiny is lack of time…time to reflect, to meditate, contemplate, pray, to be silent, receptive. Time to journal...time to wait. "The faith and the hope and the love are all in the waiting." We are invited to tell our soul to be still, and let the dark come upon you...one is encouraged to "wait without hope, for hope would be for the wrong thing...love would be love for the wrong thing..." and eventually; "The darkness will be the light, and the stillness the dancing."

It is out of this philosophy-of-life that I see or hear a still small voice, regarding the next step and the next. It might be much easier and quicker to "surf-the-net', get answers to life's questions, find a mate—or whatever else might suit one's needs...or lead to further questions. It depends entirely on your own, individual philosophy as to how you get from 'here' to 'there'. Each of us must learn, somehow, where we want to go and what vehicle we want to employ. It is a personal choice.

Taking a Mental Picture

ne really never knows what a day may bring. As we see people around us, we do not begin to comprehend what they might be experiencing. The stark reality of what can happen to a person is graphically

*T.S. Eliot's, Four Quartetts

described in the media—lost homes and loved ones through fire, flood, tornadoes, volcanoes, earthquakes, guns, bombs, and disease. But we rarely know and touch the person in the news who suffers devastation.

When my children were in elementary school, I'd wave to them as they headed toward the school bus. I'd wonder, more often than not, "Will they return? Will I see them again? Will some tragedy intervene in our lives before the day's end?" This did not make me fearful, as some people might infer. Rather it seemed a means of preparation as I committed them and myself, and our world into God's care. I'd take a mental picture of my children, and reflect on that picture throughout the day. I was aware that doing this did not insure me that nothing "bad" would happen. It was a small ritual just to make that daily imprint on my mind regarding the fragility of our lives.

When my mother was still alive and living in her own home in Little Falls, the same questions posed themselves. I remember one time vividly. As we drove away from her, I watched her force her aged body to stand and walk down her front steps in order to see us a little longer. Her weak arms waved to us. I recall wondering if I would see her again. Or was I seeing her for the last time? Would this be my last memory, my last picture of her? Was she thinking the same questions?

Happily, nothing terrible suddenly intervened in my children's young lives and they grew up into adulthood. But eventually my mother came to live with us and to die in our home. She brought transition into our daily lives. She allowed us to witness, up close, the sacredness, the gift, the treasure in living. Throughout my life I have witnessed many tragedies. With each one, I wonder how prepared am I, and how prepared were the other people to survive catastrophe and find gratitude and respect in its wake.

In light of the many tragedies that we know about each day, it is not surprising that people focus on the horrific and down play underlying causes. For example, people miss the deep tragedy of isolation and loneliness that drives high school students to react with anger, hate, bullets, and bombs, and that makes old people lose the will to live. These two age areas seem so opposite, yet they struggle with the very same losses. They die—the young on the front pages in headlines, the old on the back page obituary column. The young driven to take others along, the old leaving a remote and sometimes long list of survivors.

As an adult, I read, for the first time, the Little House on the Prairie series by Laura Ingals Wilder. I found myself wanting to live back in that time, even when I read The Long Winter. "Why?" I asked myself, "Life was so hard back then!" But I finally concluded, after much thought, that the people in those stories pulled together, helped and cared for one another as they faced the "elements."

Now that we are, generally, more insulated from the "elements", we have also become isolated from one another. We don't seem to need others as much as people did back in the 'old days'. Generally, people nowadays want to be independent of others. We have become nuclear rather than homogenous families. We have sought to become independent instead of inter-dependent. Many of us are no longer feeling that we are part of a whole, but are now autonomous and connected to no one.

The symptoms of this arise among the young, who tend to act-out their feelings. As a prominent author stated, "They cry bullets instead of tears!" The boys and young men are the "they" who have turned into killers because they do not feel integrated into the "system", but segregated by peers and immediate family. Many are set adrift with no purpose in life, and with a strong sense of not being "needed."

This, again, is not unlike the aged. Set adrift by their children whose lives are too busy to be giving much thought to anything but their own immediate survival, the elderly live alone or in Nursing Homes. Segregated from their families and their community of origin, they lose their purpose in life thus seeing themselves as being "needed" by no one.

In the 'olden-golden days', young and old gathered together to hear the same century old stories that guided and supported each generation on the journey through life. Today, we gather around the television, and take in, not our own tribal stories, but stories of strangers—violent, horny, handsome and beautiful, superficial without depth of meaning.

These stories do influence our society in many ways—from acting out emotions to apathy. But the reality of the story is always at a distance. We have gotten ourselves into quite a mess in this fast paced age-of-technology, and we all strongly sense that there really is no quick fix. There is no fix in shifting the blame from home to school, from school to home, from children to family, and from family to children.

When our personal health fails, it is prudent to try to treat the symptoms and seek out the cause at a deeper level. I suggest that the deeper level of our national "failure to health" has to do with the loss of our own sense of value. We see ourselves as only machines or slaves, maybe only a cut above computers. We have, also, been losing a sense of community in which each and every person is an integral part. We are losing our inherent values, the simplest of which is to be more conscious of the signals we send to each other. And the most complex might be to understand and accept each encounter as an opportunity to know the other more deeply. Each one of us has our fears and uncertainties. I do not imply that the "simplest" and the "most complex" are easily accomplished. But wouldn't this be an aspiration if each of us were to aim ourselves in these directions. After all, none of us knows what a day will bring and what will be the last picture we leave in the minds and hearts of those around us.

Beauty Today—Do You See It?

This past winter, as I waited for the city bus, fluffy, white, crystalline flakes fell softly to the ground. I raised my arm to a horizontal position, and watched the flakes fall on the dark material of my coat. The delicate beauty and perfect symmetry, as well as the unique design of each flake fascinated me. Soon the bus pulled up, and I was jostled out of the world of effortless beauty and tranquility, and swept on to the bus along with the other passengers into the *real* world of commerce. But the memory remained.

A few years ago a friend told me of an encounter she had at her place of work when a fellow employee launched into a litany of complaints about the weather. When she was finished, my friend asked, "But did you notice the beauty?" "No, I guess not," responded the office worker. She had seen the ice but she had not seen that white crystalline substance adorne the bare branches of all trees and bushes. The very air was sparkling. My friend had.

These past two years, more than ever before, I've been captivated and astonished at the beauty of creation—the beauty that has been made freely available to all of us wherever our eyes might travel. The last two springs, with their various green hues of new vegetation on gentle slopes, curved hills, and sweeping valleys have delighted me. Also the plains that extend so far as to make the line of the horizon distant and thin are rich in so very many different colors.

And the sky with its hues of pinks and mauves, gold and charcoal is ever changing like a kaleidoscope.

There are also the surfaces of the lakes and rivers that are ever changing, and the sparkles that seem to dance in the air above the water. How could anyone not notice such beauty?

There is also the beauty in the faces of the children and babies that are still in awe at the new world around them that has yet to be explored…their wide, innocent eyes, their slightly open rosebud lips, their delighted responses.

There is also the beauty in the aged, well-lined faces that display character: the eyes that reveal the wisdom of years, though sometimes childlike. There's the beauty and grace of the human body that's learned to utilize every muscle such as I saw recently when the James Sewell Ballet Company preformed in Little Falls. There was such grace, and seemingly flawless perfection in their dance. There was also beauty in the expressions on their young faces. Such pure joy! One cannot help finding oneself enraptured by it all.

There is such great beauty in the world around us, depending on our focus, if we live in the moment.

Two men looked out through prison bars.

One saw mud. The other stars!

Barter

Life has loveliness to sell,
All beautiful and splendid things:
Blue waves whitened on a cliff,
Climbing fire that sways and sings,
And children's faces looking up
Holding wonder like a cup.

Life has loveliness to sell:
Music like a curve of gold,
Scent of pine tress in the rain,
Eyes that love you,
Arms that hold,
And for your spirit's still delight,
Holy thoughts that star the night

Give all you have for loveliness;
Buy it and never count the cost.
For one white hour of singing peace
Give many a year of strife well lost.
And for a breath of ecstasy,
Give all you have been or could be.

Sara Teasdale (1884-1933)

Broken Walls

One morning in mid-December I awakened to a loud crash. I got up to investigate and found that a modular bookcase that had been sitting somewhat precariously and laden with plants, figurines, as well as books, had tipped over. The contents were spread out over the floor with dirt and plants separated from their pots and the heads and one arm of my boy and girl figurines broken from their bodies. The books that I'd carefully arranged in categories were laying haphazardly. I looked at the chaos that met me that morning and walked away with the intent to gather strength to clean up the mess, being unable to handle it the first thing in the morning.

As I prepared for the day and pondered on my misfortune, I thought, as I often had, of the earthquake in Iran…the broken bodies among the rubble; the agony beyond description…beyond understanding! And I thought how people all over the world have responded to help, forgetting their differences of philosophy and politics, giving aid to their fellow human beings, breaking down walls.

I thought, also, of a friend whose neighbor's daughter was deathly sick and in a coma, and the uncertainty she'd expressed to me regarding what she could do to help. In spite of her family's protests that "people don't do that sort of thing anymore," she made meals and brought them to her neighbors—meals which were gladly received. Fear of intruding into the lives of people with whom one is barely acquainted gives way to the need to do what one can to help. Sorrow and tragedy have their way of breaking down barriers that we unwittingly erect, and we forget our differences.

But why must we always wait until tragedy strikes to be helpful to our 'neighbors', or by the same token, to receive help from our neighbor?

Why do we isolate ourselves in independence, when inter dependence might better connect us to our neighbor? Might it be that we're afraid to be vulnerable, vulnerable in what we may offer being rejected?

"Oh, no—I can't accept that!" "I can't let you do that!" And/or would being on the receiving end be too humbling? Or Obligating? Or maybe an admission that we're in need? I'm reminded of one of my all-time favorite and haunting songs from days gone by called, "Nature Boy."

> *"There was a boy, a very strange enchanted boy,*
>
> *A little shy and sad of eye, but very wise was he.*
>
> *And then one day, one magic day he passed my way*
>
> *And while we spoke of many things, fools and kings,*
>
> *This he said to me: The greatest thing you'll ever learn is just*
>
> *To love and be loved in return."*

"Simple gestures taking place on the surface of life can be of central importance to the soul."* And they can also melt the heart and break down existing barriers between us...such as a smile and nod to a stranger, or a gentle touch to the shoulder of a friend.

*Thomas Moore, Care of the Soul.

Take Time to Listen to Resolve Conflict

Last week I was introduced to a gentleman who had lived and taught school in Israel for the past five years. I asked him his perspective on the Middle East conflict. As he began to respond, I heard yelling behind me. It was from a woman who had passed by, apparently, within earshot. She was enraged by what she heard and was reacting verbally. I can't remember what she'd been saying in the beginning, only what she said as she stomped away, "You're an idiot!" His immediate response: "No, you're the idiot."

I stood in stunned silence as the two continued to exchange epithets. So volatile was the emotional climate that I feared something more than verbal exchanges might occur. It was over an hour before my breathing returned to normal.

Upon reflection, this was like a microcosm of the macrocosm of the Middle East crisis. Each person projecting evil intent on the other, not willing to say, "Let's talk this over in a reasonable manner, let's try to listen to each other and see if we can resolve this issue between us.

Upon further reflection, I realized the impossibility of my making a judgment regarding the rightness or wrongness of either party. In the same way, I find it impossible to sort out truth from inaccuracies, fact from fiction, all I can do is be willing to listen and try to understand the history that's created such division between the people in conflict and have compassion for both.

I've listened to radio and watched interviews on some of the TV programs and find that the ones who are the easiest to "listen" to are those who seek to understand both sides of the conflict. Listening. Compassion. These are the keys...non-judgmental concern. This can send balm to Gilead.

... To Fulfill the Dream

lthough I've never learned to ice-skate, it has been a fascination of mine since I was very young. Whenever I developed a 'crush' on a boy, I'd fantasize that we were ice-skating together. Sonja Henie was the skater that had inspired me in those days. She was possibly the first skater to bring the drama and romance of ice-skating to the movies and wide public attention.

My fascination of ice-skating has been renewed in the past several years as I've watched the skating competitions on TV. There are no 'crushes' on which to focus my attention, but my deep appreciation of ice-skating has greatly increased as I become more sensitive to beauty, grace, and form of the various skaters. They seem to skate with such ease. And yet I'm keenly aware that the ease with which they glide and jump and spin has been earned at great cost, great sacrifice. When I watch a triple lutz and a perfect, graceful landing, I often wonder at the many times they must have tried and failed, suffering painful falls before their triumph. So many bruises, torn muscles, and broken bones—not to mention disappointment and humiliation.

Therefore, I've come to have great admiration for these beautiful, vibrant, vigorous people-with-a-passion. I admire their hard work and tenacity, as I think of the hours and days and months and years that have gone into one glorious, shining performance.

And there is something else I've come to hold in high esteem—their ability to get right up and go on when they fall. What a potent image that is to me. I sit in my comfortable chair, as I watch those spills, and suffer pain for them (they work so hard!) and marvel at the way they get right up and keep going with the music. They don't seem to miss a beat. And yet, the disappointment shows in their faces when the performance is over. I've also seen the joy and triumph written on the faces of those who know that they gave an almost flawless performance.

And then…I reflect on how these beautiful skaters and their passion for their work can be a metaphor of life. There is the Passion; there is the goal; there is the Dream; there is the one bright 'shining moment' of Camelot. There is, behind and before the glory of achievement, the commitment to a great love—a love so great that enormous sacrifice is required to fulfill the Dream.

And then…I wonder, Am I willing to be 'impregnated' with a vital Dream? How willing am I to pay the high price of failure, of trial and error as I move toward my own unique goal? Can I bear the pain of falling, bruising, and humiliation as I move out into the next challenge that the year ahead might bring if I dare to risk?

And then...I think of those beautiful skaters and draw fresh inspiration.

(Note: Sonja Henie was the first female skater to win Olympic Gold medals. She won in 1928, 1932, and 1936.)

It's about Caring...

I've begun in the past few years, or so, to take real interest in the Academy Awards Presentations. I've talked to myself about this. I've been somewhat of a snob, in the past, about watching anything on TV. It's made me smile and sometimes chuckle over the way we've all explained ourselves when we want to tell someone about an item on TV.

If we're important people with important things to do, TV watching might ruin our image of ourselves. We think we don't have time for such trivia and paint with a broad brush in order to minimize any value that a particular program might have to offer. I've done that. I know that some of you must have done that also.

After talking with myself about this new found interest that I may spend too much time alone, I've concluded that a program such as the Academy Awards presentations offers me the opportunity to view people who have worked hard at their art, being honored for it. It's inspired me, and I have a great desire for inspiration. I've come to realize that I have this desire because I don't see enough people in the real world who strive to be good at what they do. I see a lot of shortcutting to get the job done so it's just barely good enough. Whatever the job whether manual labor or the world of the arts or of politics one can always strive to do ones very best. Passion for one's work seems often to be missing.

My mother had a passion for the simple task of folding laundered clothes. She used to show me how to fold clothes..."and then press with your hands." As she neatly folded sheets and towels, and whatever else should get folded. Her admonitions stuck! I like folding clothes neatly, and I always hear her voice, "now press with your hands..." She also took pleasure in ironing, smoothing out the wrinkles with a hot iron. These were small areas of seeking perfection but important nonetheless.

Another lesson I learned from a young friend who lived in our home and helped me care for my invalid mother was how to set a table. I came home one evening to a cloth covered table with cloth napkins, fresh flowers and candlelight. It made a great impression on me. It was thoughtfully done and I have followed her example for the last 20 years because of how much it meant to me. (Thank you, Therese, wherever you are!) To create an ambiance into which another can step and feel honored is well worth the small, extra effort.

To strive to be one's best and become good at whatever one does is a way of saying, "I truly care!" Sure, some people do the same thing just for 'show,' but that isn't what I'm talking about. It's about caring. It's about living one's life symbolically, it's pressing out wrinkles of life and setting up atmospheres to express our love though the way we do what we do. We may win no awards, but there's always someone in our audience of friends and family who will remember our performance and delight in our efforts. Whatever the job, whether manual labor or the world of the arts or politics, one can strive to do one's best. One's best isn't always someone else's best, to be sure. But passion for one's work seems often to be missing.

"...Small Things with Great Love"

The September/October issues of the Good Earth Newsletter carried the story of a guest writer, Jerry Wellik. He told of a former teacher of his who approached him the night of his graduation with a word of encouragement, saying, "Jerry, you can do anything you decide you want to do."

That simple gesture made an impact on Jerry, both that night and in the years to come. So deeply touched was he that he remembered what Rod Hatle (his teacher) had said to him thirty-five years later when memories were being shared at a class reunion. The result of this treasured memory took the form of a telephone call to his former teacher with words of appreciation for the weight of influence those words carried.

I was reminded of Jerry's story when I thought of Mother Teresa's life-long motto: "Do small things with great love."

Mother Teresa has *moved on* but the power of her influence on others lives on and her motto ripples out into a world hungry for love, needy for sensitive touch, and sick of the pressures and pace of society.

Many various activities connected to the holidays of the next two months begin to unfold, carrying with them joys and agonies. Along with anticipation of the added pressure of what is expected of us by others and what we expect of ourselves, we are in need of some valuable guidelines to help us direct our desires, energies, and expectations.

Here and now, before the holidays are upon us and we begin to feel pressed into doing more, buying more, expecting more of ourselves and others than budget and wisdom should allow, let's engage in a little reflection on the intangible gifts that we've received over the years. Let us take time to sit down and open up our large or small box of treasured memories…gifts of others that have lasted through the years. Gifts that don't go out of style, don't break or wear out, gifts that keep on giving—small things done with great love.

These are gifts that can be shared with others, as Jerry did in his story of his teacher, celebrating his memory by making that phone call and expressing his appreciation for his teacher's kind words and then writing that poignant story and poem.

Which gifts have the most meaning for you throughout your life—tangible or intangible? Give this some thought. Find your memories, choose a quiet evening and reminisce, reflect, and recall with others because in this time of pausing you use your greatest treasures and give the wealthiest presents.

Speaking Our Own Truth

Throughout the past months the subject, "How do we, as individuals, perceive the many situations as they arise in the process of life?" has presented itself in many ways and in many forms.

Some examples of this subject about which we all have an opinion are: (a) the weather, (b) the impeachment trials of President Clinton, (c) the Y2K problem.

The weather comes up more often maybe because it's a safe subject. However we end a conversation, we seem to begin with the weather. Weather is the mood of the world. And we need weather, good or bad, as a healing sympathizer to our feelings or overt expresser of our mood. The weather serves us in many more ways than we know. We might cast our vote for a sunny or dreary day, depending on our mood. Through the years at the Co-op I have heard a variety of opinions and perceptions about the weather.

Opinions on the weather belong to the people that offer them, and an opinion can be judged as neither right nor wrong, accurate or inaccurate. However, I do often make an attempt to remind people, "This is Minnesota; what do you expect?" Or I may say, "It could be worse!" And sometimes I respond with, "Accept what is." The main goal is to bring some balance to what I see in others as a lopsided view or outlook.

Because I have this goal of balance I may be perceived as judgmental and accusatory. I do not mean to judge or accuse. I do mean to offer another perspective, one that the other person has perhaps not thought of. I have wondered, "Is a perspective wrong and right?" Because I have one perspective, do I have the right to call another 'wrong' or 'limited?' Among friends, I feel that it is my honor-bound duty to make every attempt possible to share what I believe to be 'right.' I believe in my perspective.

But it is also my honor-bound duty to listen thoroughly to the other person, to hear their perspective on what he/she sees. I can do this! I can even involve some degree of respect for another person's perspective. Hopefully as a result of this exchange, I can move through our dialogue without feeling that I must convince the other person that I am right and he/she is wrong. I hope that, as a result of this exchange, we both learn something that aids in bringing better understanding and balance rather than a solution to the discussion.

The impeachment trial of President Clinton and the Y2K problem are topics that produce stronger opinions than the weather. Many people have grown weary and troubled by the constant barrage of information from media coverage. Division and derision exist in congressional leadership and among experts. People feel misguided and mis-informed. There are no clear answers but everyone has an opinion.

As we all face the realm of the unknown: we have the opportunity to share our views, our own perspective, without shooting down another's view and perspective. If we can listen with receptivity and respect, opinion exchanges can be mutually beneficial and help us all keep an open mind. We can learn from the other person, we can gain humility; we can see through different eyes and gain a new perspective, as we avail ourselves of the opportunity of a variety of viewpoints.

Isn't much of the problem that arises between us, as conflicts arise (and they always do), that we haven't heard the whole story or that we can't place any value on the possibility that there is a valid other side? To be willing to listen to others, to hear each other out, may not only bring more balance to our perceptions and perspectives, but it may break down the barriers that exist between us and our fellow human beings.

As barriers are dissolved in an atmosphere of respect and receptivity, there may emerge a stronger bond between us even though we may continue to disagree on subjects we discuss.

I'm reminded of a little saying that caught my attention long ago: "Although I may not agree with what you say, I will defend to my death your right to say it."

In the midst of the turmoil of the world's conflicts, wouldn't it be a good idea for us to give each other the right to speak one's own truth as we each see that truth, whether it concerns the weather, the impeachment, or Y2K. Let's not shoot down or discredit each other. Let's hear each other out. The only possible danger might be a paradigm shift.

Time Well Spent

I keep a journal. I've journaled for many years. In the distant past I tried to begin journaling, but my good intentions fell by the wayside. Maybe it was because I just didn't know how! I didn't know what to keep and what to throw away, what to say and how to say it.

Inspiration came to me when I read the journals, put into book form, of Etty Hillesum. They were called <u>The Diary of Etty Hillesum</u> and. They tell the story of a young Jewish woman who lived and died during the Holocaust. Her writing was honest, inspiring, and meaty, from her gut. She didn't, in any way, depict a "victim" attitude. Maybe that's one of the things that impressed me the most about her writing. She had a shining spirit that shone through the dark clouds that had descended on Germany in those tormented times.

I marveled at how she held up—a noble soul who seemed to have delved deeply into the depths of the darkness and sorrows that plagued the Jewish people in those times and came up with gold! And maybe one of the reasons she held up so well was in the fact that she kept a diary.

I've learned, as I've written in my journal through these past years, that the thoughts which sometimes keep swimming around in my mind could be anchored down in my journal and not keep on tormenting me. This is not to say that my mind would be completely free of troubling thoughts but journaling has been a great help. This documentation of my life, its joys and sorrows, hills and valleys has been a means of unburdening myself to this "friend." This "friend" of whom

I speak often gives me feedback simply through the validation of who I am and what I'm about. An unwritten rule of my journaling—a self-inflicted rule—is that I must be honest about what's going on in my life and what I'm feeling at the time. This isn't always easy. It has, in fact, kept me from entries for days at a time. I haven't always wanted to be honest with myself and my "friend." There had been times when I wanted to just put things out of my mind, dump them into the oblivion of the unconscious with little hope of resolution…just make it all go away! A journal…at least for a non-Catholic, could be called a "confessional," at which time, I could receive absolution through admitting where I've gone wrong, forgive myself as well as receive God's forgiveness, for the things that have caused me great regret. I don't want to defend myself but simply own what I've done and what I feel, without excuse. Sometimes I find I need to rectify the issue by asking someone else's forgiveness. Everything becomes more crystallized when experiences are put in writing to be re-read when the emotion of the moment has become subdued.

One customer told me of an interesting book titled <u>Emotions Buried Alive Never Die</u>. It's a provocative title in that we all can recognize the truth contained in that title. It has become a long-standing belief of mine that emotions buried alive can cause very concrete pain in the body as well as disturbances in the mind. I've had such experiences where I've addressed emotional problems and then experienced freedom from bodily pain. At such times when the freedom from pain is realized it is confirmed to me that "my issues were in my tissues."

Some people tell me, when I encourage them to journal, that one of the greatest fears in keeping a journal is that someone might find it and read it. Or that they might die without being able to destroy their journal. My response is, "Why?"

I desire to have the people close to me know me for who I am. But I desire people to be *interested* in me—not just curious. Also, I want to know who I am, and when I read old journals of mine, it affords me that opportunity. In this way, I've found, I can be-friend myself, as I read in those pages what I have gone through, how I handled things at a different time, how I actually felt. I gain insight into the psyche of myself as though viewing another person with desires and disappointments, trials, and failures, hopes and joy, the pain of her pilgrimage on this earth, and the transfiguring joy that emerges through the pain, through her belief that "all things are working together for good—The Higher Good."

Florida Scott Maxwell wrote a journal-like book titled Measure of My Days, in which she evaluates her life with the wisdom of the aged—like good wine ready to be tasted and savored. She seems to seek where she is on life's map. I'm thankful for the 'journaling' of her life that's benefited me.

Keeping a journal has been beneficial in writing these articles for the Newsletter as I go into the depths. And ask, "What subject are we on for now?" and then draw upon the thoughts that have begun to accumulate in the psyche that can be shared, always with the hope that they might give the reader pause to think and reflect. Sometimes it feels like there's nothing there. But I wait until something begins to emerge—rise up as if from an enveloping fluid. This takes time, yet time well spent.

An Alternative Medicine's Contribution to Modern Medicine

We seem now to be moving out of an era where we sought answers to mental, emotional, and physical problems outside of ourselves. We've sought knowledgeable 'experts' who would tell us what to do and how to do it. Mostly we've been pumped full of various pills and medicines that have often created side effects that are worse than the disease and we die due to their cumulative effects. We have come to believe in the 'quick-fix' approach to our various maladies, and we have paid dearly for this folly. Many of us have, as a result, become disillusioned with the 'experts who tell us what's what and have begun taking responsibility for our own lives.

The resulting burden of responsibility of our own lives has driven us within ourselves for answers. Many of us have found resources we hadn't before comprehended. A unique consciousness about our own lives. And Lo and behold! Life in general continues to unfold." The methods of healing that were employed were of minimal nature—simple activities such as suggestion, talking, touching, or being silent in order to help the sick person. These tools involved a certain way of being." So says Larry Dossey, M.D. So much of our need, whether mental, physical, emotional, or spiritual, lies in being. We need time, we need rest, and we need space in order to work through our problems. We also need support of friends and family.

But there are many people, sad to say, who continue to buy into the quick fix approach, simply give into the pressure of time. However, these people who are having a race with time are realizing that a quick fix is only an illusion, and the fix isn't long lasting. Therefore, we must simply take time to seek the meaning in the various illnesses that move into our bodies, and our minds and our neighborhoods, and our communities. These illnesses are messengers, and we haven't always taken time to stop and read the message they bear. We treat the symptoms but don't seek the cause…like disconnecting the smoke alarm when it sends out its messages while the fire rages on.

Dr. Dossey stated, "…Let us take a look at modern medicine. Modern Medicine is a here-and-now term. It implies a medicine that is recent, up-to-date, contemporary, and 'now' as opposed to ancient, antiquated and old-fashioned. Our concept of 'modern' requires a linear time, a time in which the 'now' is safely walled off from the past and future, the flowing time of common sense."*

*Meaning and Medicine by Larry Dosse

Common sense is such a comfortable, old-fashioned, basic term. Common sense, according to Aristotle, is "to know what's true." Knowing what's true comes as a result of being, waiting, listening for messages from within ourselves to come to the surface. It requires allowing time and space for the unconscious within us to become conscious. It is as if we're giving birth to the truth from within ourselves—often accompanied by labor pains.

We need not abandon seeking information and help from the 'experts' as we turn inward for that inner wisdom that each individual among us possesses. Balance comes into play here. We need to balance what comes to us as a result of being open to all sources of truth and then sorting through the information.

So let us mine the gold and other treasures that lay hidden in the deep crevices and caves of our unconscious being. Let's tune into some of that ancient wisdom that fosters common sense. We may not always find a cure, but we're more likely to find a healing.

Perspectives on Cinderella

I recently watched yet another version of Cinderella titled: <u>Ever After</u>, starring Drew Barrymore as Cinderella. The role Drew played was not the long-suffering, meek and obedient Cinderella I've grown use to. Oh, no, this Cinderella had spunk! She was tough—she was strong! And she wasn't about to allow those evil stepsisters and that evil stepmother to dominate her—at least not without some resistance. This version of Cinderella simply wasn't going to fall into the role of victim. No one was gonna' push <u>her</u> around!

In describing the above version of a more modern-day Cinderella—it must not be assumed that I negate the value of the Cinderella I've become the most familiar with through the years. Where, the new version had spunk, the 'time tested' Cinderella possessed patience. Patience is an admirable quality in a person, especially when one realizes the great value of patience: a quiet waiting that develops into endurance bringing about an inner strength that can withstand the trials that life hands us.

There are times when spunk comes to our rescue in difficult situations…times when we seem required to stand our ground. I think of spunk as a spontaneous response, and we need to be ready in certain situations to lay claim to that form of decisive action. Some of us need a little more spunk while some of us need to curtail that attitude at times.

We need the patience that serves to develop inner strength that steadies us and yields to the needs of others.

> "Hold steady where the fires burn,
>
> When inner lessons come to learn,
>
> And from this path seems no turn—
>
> Let patience have her perfect work."

The spunky Cinderella or the patient Cinderella? Or maybe a little balance between the two? Let the reader decide.

Pay No Attention to the Man Behind the Curtain, Unless...!

And just who is the man behind the curtain? I surmise that he's a man who's developed a fearsome persona to compensate for his lack of a well-developed sense of identity. But isn't there much more to the man behind the curtain when he becomes exposed by a little dog?

The 'doggie,' Toto, isn't unlike the little boy in The Emperor's New Clothes who cut through the pretense of those around him, and the sham of the Emperor's display of pretended finery. The boy was completely innocent in his honest response—and spoke what he knew to be true. In his astonishment at seeing his naked Emperor, he called it as he saw it, and burst forth with the naked truth—possessing no sense of proper etiquette in the given situation. He had no idea of how important pretense in a social situation was. He had no idea of social acceptability...and how necessary to just go-with-the-flow of things. But did you doubt for a minute he set the 'flow' in a new direction? I didn't. As the truth marched forth in the form of a child—the crowd, as well as the Emperor, had to have realized the 'jig was up!' What embarrassment that little boy had caused...to everyone! Or so it seems. Or, on the other hand, what embarrassment the Emperor caused for himself by pretending something that was not true. The author doesn't tell us what came next. It might be an interesting project to write our own conclusion to the story.

In the story of the Wizard of Oz we're given a much clearer picture of the man behind the curtain: He's a peddler, the author depicts, when Dorothy first meets up with him…a kind man, sharing his food with the doggie that would ultimately expose him…when he asserted himself to be something he was not. He was also shy and uncertain (it must be assumed from the author's depiction) stumbling over his words, hesitant and maybe feeling some degree of inferiority due to his low position in life.

However, similar to the story of the Emperor's New Clothes, an insignificant little dog became the vehicle for exposing the truth that the Great Wizard of Oz was only a persona. Yet behind the persona was a man who seemed to have meant well…a person who wanted to aid the weary travelers in their individual quests (he, too, was a traveler). But unlike the boy in the Emperor's New Clothes, the child Dorothy scolds him. "Shame on You!" she asserts.

However, when the Great Wizard had been properly exposed and then shamed, we find that underneath all the sham is a wise and kind soul with the gift of helping others recognize the gold within themselves, one who is able to meet need in a variety of ways. But as he assessed each individual quest, it was his confidence that each one of them already possessed what they'd been seeking outside of themselves! He directed them inward to their own inner resources.

It's such a simple truth…so simple that we often fail to comprehend it. So simple that we can't see it "except we become as a child…" It's a gift that can only be received by the lowly and humble of heart. It's a gift! But it becomes our gift when we drop the sham.

Pay no attention to the man behind the 'curtain' unless you're seeking wisdom. Pay no attention to the little boy in the crowd, unless you're seeking truth.

The Nun and I

As I boarded the bus to Minneapolis I observed that one-third of a front seat was empty. A nun (in full habit) occupied the other two-thirds and was obviously trying to save other seat for herself. She was not a large woman and scarcely needed one of the seats. Since a front seat was my ideal choice, and since all the other seats were occupied by at least one other person, I chose to claim that almost free front seat. I leaned over and asked, "Is this seat taken?" She either didn't hear me or wished to ignore me. I repeated the question a little more firmly. Without answering or looking up she moved off the partially occupied seat, and I sat down.

It hadn't been a hospitable gesture, I thought, I'm not really welcome here. However, I claimed the space I had purchased and trusted that God would mediate between us—somewhat hoping that we might at least speak a word or two to one another.

As I opened the book that I'd brought along, I thought that, possibly, she might glance over at it as I've often done when someone pulls out a book. She may recognize the Catholic author, Hubert Van Zeller. And even the chapter I was reading, "Sanctity and Environment" and realize that here was a person on a spiritual search. But if she cast any sidelong glance, I wasn't aware of it.

I read, "I think of the mercy of God as a sudden melting of an attitude that was intending to be stern…of the generosity of God as dealing out gifts from an inexhaustible store."

Here we sit—two women. Me in my bare shoulders and legs, dressed in a colorful skirt and she in her black habit, fully covered with only her face and hands revealed—nothing else. We sit here side by side, two women, not speaking or communicating in any observable way.

I yield myself to you, God, and trust that your will might be fulfilled in this trip. Yes, I can understand how difficult my outer appearance might be for her to accept, but outer appearance means nothing; help her to realize that. I've come to realize that through the many experiences through which you've led me.

What was she thinking? I glanced sidelong at her. She seemed to be watching the bus driver. I look at the driver. His manner does seem a bit odd as he seems to thrash about in his seat. He'd been so very abrupt and sarcastic with me when I asked him if this was the bus to Minneapolis. Now, as I became addicted to watching him as my fellow passenger had been, I thought, *Is he on something? How trusting,* I thought, *we are of these bus drivers, pilots, conductors, etc. We don't give a second thought to any question of their competence.* I begin to become tense as I observe his jerky motions. I thought of the captain of the Valdez and his apparent incompetence—his abdication! I, then, was reminded by a gentle nudging from the deep recesses of my being that I was in God's hands—*If I perish, I perish! Why be afraid if I'm in his will?* I remembered the resource of prayer—praying for the driver, for myself, for the nun, my fellow passengers—asking God to fill the entire bus with His spirit. My driver-watching addiction was broken, and I closed my eyes in peace and rest and safety. The passengers were so quiet, I noticed.

Later I read some more. I watched the countryside swim by and the city with all its directional signs begin to appear on the horizon. Almost there!

The driver picked up his microphone and announced that we were entering Minneapolis. He told those whose destination was Chicago to return to this bus. He asked us to remain seated until the bus stopped. He sounded very sane and sensible. Maybe he'd been in pain. Maybe moving around in his seat helped him alleviate a problem with tense muscle spasms. Maybe I'd misjudged him…as I often tend to misjudge others.

We pulled into the dimly lit terminal. My 'friends,' I could see, were waiting in their parked car. It's so good to have someone meeting you at your destination. (This has a deeper meaning, as all things in life do.) I was so happy to see that they were there!

The bus stops. The nun and I both have our satchels on our laps, waiting. I stand up, step into the aisle and step back, deferring to her. She, too, steps into the aisle and without a word or gesture, debarks.

Hers was, perhaps, a hidden life. So much so, that her in-tune-ness with God, her intercession for the driver and her fellow passengers made her forget the social graces. What can one know from outward appearances?

Epilogue

It's been a joy to share these treasures I've found beneath the *stones* of my life…some, which I stumbled upon, and some that I've almost stumbled over.

I've become somewhat addicted to *treasure* hunting…in seeking the meaning that has lain beneath the various events of my seventy-two years. I've found in seeking meaning I've been able to heartily agree with the Apostle Paul, who offered me great hope in the words he wrote, "…and we know that all things work together for good for those who love God…"

My hope in offering this collection of essays is that you, the reader, will seek the deeper meaning of the things and events that unfold in *your* life— "*lest you have the experience but miss the meaning.*"

Thank you for being receptive to the images I've found through the Lens of my perceptions.

Footnote

As I walked the three block trek to the place I would chose as my publisher, I thought of the thousands of times I've made that little journey. You see—the place that Mk Publishing now occupies was the place that the Good Earth Food Coop once occupied for many years. The place where I was general manager for over seven years. The place where these essays for the Good Earth Newsletter were first published and distributed. It's a place of many treasured memories of a community of beautiful, sensitive people that I've grown to love and cherish more and more as years go by. Dear People, I thank God for you!

Order form

Name: _____

address: _____

city: _____

State: _____ ZIP: _____

Phone: _____

Mail order form to:

_____ Copies at $11.95 ea. $ _____

METAMORPHOSIS
222 3RD AVE NE
ST CLOUD MN 56304

Free Shipping & Handling

Total $ _____

Please remit by check, M.O. or Bank Draft. Please make check payable to:
Phyllis Feia. Thank you.